In Other Words . . .

12 Short Stories Based On New Testament Parables

Merle G. Franke

CSS Publishing Company, Inc.
Lima, Ohio

IN OTHER WORDS ...

Copyright © 1993 by
The CSS Publishing Company, Inc.
Lima, Ohio

All rights reserved. No part of this publication may be reproduced, stored in a retrieval system, or transmitted in any form or by any means, electronic, mechanical, photocopying, recording, or otherwise, without the prior permission of the publisher. Inquiries should be addressed to: The CSS Publishing Company, Inc., 628 South Main Street, Lima, Ohio 45804.

Library of Congress Cataloging-in-Publication Data

Franke, Merle G., 1924-
  In other words — : 12 short stories based on New Testament parables / by Merle G. Franke.
    p.   cm.
  ISBN 1-55673-635-5
  1. Christian fiction, American. 2. Jesus Christ — Parables — Fiction. I. Title.
PS3556.R334615   1993
813'.54—dc20   93-28214
                                                                CIP

9359 / ISBN 1-55673-635-5   PRINTED IN U.S.A.

*This Book Is Dedicated Primarily
To My Family:
My wife Virginia
My five children and six grandchildren
And to the many parishioners I have
served through the years.*

Table Of Contents

Foreword — 7

Impatient Planter — 9
  Matthew 13:1-23
  The Sower

A Question Of Identity — 19
  Matthew 13:24-30, 36-43
  The Weeds Among The Wheat

Role Model Ignored — 27
  Matthew 18:23-35
  The Unforgiving Servant

The Contractor's Choice — 37
  Matthew 20:1-16
  The Laborers In The Vineyard

The Bishop And The Lady — 45
  Luke 7:36-50
  A Sinful Woman Forgiven

Neighbor To The Man — 53
  Luke 10:25-37
  The Good Samaritan

Midas — 59
  Luke 12:13-21
  The Rich Fool

I've Heard That Song Before — 67
  Luke 14:16-24
  The Great Dinner

Which Ones Were Lost? 73
    Luke 15:1-10
    The Lost Sheep, Coins

A Woman Had Two Daughters ... 81
    Luke 15:11-32
    The Prodigal Son

Blind In One Eye ... 93
    Luke 16:19-31
    The Rich Man And Lazarus

Perfect In Every Way 101
    Luke 18:9-14
    Pharisee And Tax Collector

Foreword

How do you read the parables of the New Testament? Or how do you hear them read at a worship service or Bible study? If you are like the average person who is somewhat familiar with the most well-known parables that Jesus told, you most likely know in advance what the point of the parable is — or the moral of the story. The reason you know the point of the parable is that you've heard it many times over. You are familiar with the Good Samaritan and the Prodigal Son and many others, so that you might nod your head in agreement with the parable even while it is being read.

Yet there remains something different about the parables. Perhaps it is the setting or the circumstances. And quite often it is the cast of characters. Most of us are not familiar with the circumstances of lost sheep or a pharisee and a publican in the temple praying. No one would argue that these and other parables are excellent stories, but they are set in a time and circumstances with which we are not familiar. The parable of the workers in the vineyard, for instance, is made up of a scenario and circumstances that are different from our contemporary society. Most people today are not familiar with workers in the vineyard, and certainly not with workers getting paid at the end of each work day. For us the characters of the parables might be like antiques — we appreciate their uniqueness and distinctive features, but they don't live with us. We see them as from afar.

Not so with the people in Jesus' day who heard the parables first hand. Jesus used examples and settings and characters out of the real life of his time. His listeners were familiar with vineyards and shepherds and planting crops by throwing the seeds by hand. For them the characters and scenarios jumped out at them with instant recognition. They knew, for instance, the dangers of travellers going down from Jerusalem to Jericho. But because that's not a scene with which we easily identify, we can only assume that it was a hazardous trip. Nevertheless, while the characters and settings of the New Testament are placed in antiquity, the parables remain strong teaching tools for us.

But suppose one were to retell — or "translate" — some of the New Testament parables by placing them in contemporary settings with contemporary characters, to make them as familiar to us as they were to Jesus' listeners. Could we not more quickly identify with the story and its intended moral if the characters and scenario jumped off the page at us as we read them? Familiar sounding characters, familiar sounding circumstances. The idea of rewriting some of the parables in this fashion was not original with me. I had heard a friend of mine read a parable that had been rewritten and placed in a contemporary setting. And I began studying once again the New Testament parables to see how many of them would lend themselves to such a retelling.

The scriptural parables are valuable and treasured stories in their own right. This collection of 12 short stories is an attempt to tell them again, in other words; to create modern parallel parables. I have retold 11 of the parables plus one incident in the life of Jesus. Most of them are set in the 1990s, in settings and with characters that will likely be familiar to readers. Each parable is given a contemporary title, but the original parable is indicated with its scriptural reference, so that readers may first read the parable from scripture, then the story based on it. That's the sequence I recommend. The intent, of course, is to highlight the same point or moral that is being made in the scriptural version of the parable.

The book title *In Other Words* . . . was suggested by my long-time colleague in ministry Steve Youngdahl, who has been a valuable critic of my writing in the past.

Merle G. Franke
Austin, Texas

Impatient Planter

Parallel Parable: Matthew 13:1-23
The Sower

"I guess I wanted to be a preacher from the time I was a little kid." It was the newly-ordained Cal Thompson talking to his new friend and fellow pastor, John Childress. The age difference between the two of them was more than a generation, Cal having been ordained less than six months, and John over the 40-year mark. It wasn't exactly a natural friendship that was forming; instead it was a pairing of two pastors arranged by the conference dean. A new program had been in effect for a couple years, a program in which newly-ordained pastors who came into synod were paired with an older and more experienced pastor who acted as a mentor to the young one. The program was called "peer partners," and its intention was that the two would meet from time to time so that the older pastor could share his experience and accumulated wisdom with the newcomer. And in most cases in synod it seemed to be having fairly good results. The new young pastors needed someone with whom they could share their frustrations and anxieties, and get some good sound advice from time to time about the realities of parish life.

"You wanted to be a preacher or an all-around pastor? There is often a difference, depending how much emphasis you put in one place or another." John was not only seeking clarification, but was hoping to draw young Cal into some thoughtful conversation. John had seen plenty of young pastors come and go through his years in the ministry, and often in the past he wished he would have had an opportunity to sit down with some of them and pick their brains.

He wasn't always sure they knew which way they wanted to go in the ministry. That plus the fact that those newly-ordained pastors, particularly the younger ones, often were so idealistic that John had the urge to bring them gently down to earth a bit.

Cal wasn't so idealistic as to render him impractical, but his eagerness and enthusiasm caught John's attention early on in their peer partnership, and John wanted to make sure that eagerness would be directed in the way that would make Cal's ministry as effective as possible. Cal responded, "Well, sure, I wanted to be a pastor; but I've always been particularly attracted to the preaching aspect of it."

"What attracted you to preaching?" John wanted to know.

"I don't know for sure. I can't put my finger on it exactly," Cal answered after thinking about it for a few seconds. "All I can say is that from the time I was a young teenager I was moved — and I guess impressed — by the preaching of my own pastor. And all through seminary my interest in preaching was strengthened and supported. I suppose you might say I really want to plant the Word. Is that too naive?"

"No, it's not naive at all. It's great," John allowed, "But you need to be aware of the fact that your preaching is the one place in your ministry where it's the most difficult to measure results. That is, if it's results you're looking for."

"Well, of course we all want to see results from what we do," Cal noted, then paused to consider how to follow up on that. "I can't put it in any profound manner. I simply want to be a planter of God's Word and see what happens, see some growth take place. I am a firm believer in the power of the planted Word to change people."

"Of course, you should be, otherwise you'd be in the wrong calling," John said. "I just want to caution you about having your expectations too high in terms of that preached Word changing people according to your time table. You have a right to expect big things to happen, but you also will need some patience — and some reality as to how the Word works."

"How does it work?" Cal couldn't help but ask that with a slight smile.

And John took it as gentle kidding. They were going to get along just fine in this peer partnership. "When I find out, I'll let you know," John said.

"I've got to hit the road, John," Cal said as he glanced at his watch, "I've got my first funeral tomorrow and I've got to see the family again this afternoon. Same time next month?"

"Fine by me. I'll have the coffee pot on again," John said as he walked to the door with Cal. "Oh, and don't forget to plant the Word . . . at the funeral and on Sunday."

"Thanks, John."

That had been their second meeting as peer partners, and now the month between this and their next meeting had flown by. Cal was already acquainted with the time demands on a parish pastor, and he was concerned about his sermon preparation time getting threatened by things they hadn't told him about in seminary. Cal was genuinely looking forward to these monthly meetings with his older colleague. It was kind of like having a private tutor. And while John questioned Cal closely about his (Cal's) strong opinions, John never seemed to be critical of him. And unlike seminary, Cal didn't have to depend on John for his grade points, so he could unload as he pleased.

"What do you think of this church growth business, John? I've been in conversation with some gung ho pastors who seem to be all caught up in the business of making their congregations grow until they're the biggest in town."

John paused, "Well, I don't think there's anything wrong with growth. And after all, if you're the planter, you want to plant the Word in as many people as possible, right?" He didn't wait for an answer. "But I think the more important question is, what is the motivation for growth? Unfortunately there are a lot of pastors who appear to be more interested in their own reputations as "successful" pastors than in what it means to be a faithful pastor."

"Can't they be both?" Cal asked.

"Maybe so," John replied, "But I have the feeling that when the Word is preached in its truth and purity — as Brother Martin would have us do — it isn't always going to bring, or at least maintain, the large crowds."

"What do you think people want to hear?" Cal asked, but almost instantly wished he hadn't. It was almost too juvenile a question.

John thought a moment before replying. "I recall some years ago that some of my colleagues in ministry told me that I could fill my church to overflowing every Sunday if only I would tell people what they wanted to hear. You'll recall from your Old Testament studies that Jeremiah fussed about the false prophets doing that. And that's a real temptation — tell 'em what they want to hear. But good preaching doesn't depend upon what people want to hear. You know that, I don't have to tell you that."

"I knew you'd say that about preaching, but it's good to hear it anyway," Cal said, and was interrupted ....

"You say the right buzz words, tickle their funny bone once in a while, spout some pious sounding innocuous stuff, you might be able to draw the crowds. But I thought you wanted to plant the Word. Tell me if I'm wrong," John concluded, thinking he might have stepped on Cal's toes a bit. But why stop now? He'd been doing that in his preaching for 40 years.

Both men drained their second cup of coffee. Cal looked at his watch and mumbled he had to get back to work.

John commented about the watch-looking, "I think pastors look at their watch more than at their Bible — and I suspect some of them pay more attention to the watch. But I'm talking from experience; I've been looking at my watch 50 times a day for 40 years. And you'll be doing the same. Let's both get back to work, and next time I'll come over to your place."

"Great! I'll show you some of the stuff we're planning," Cal said as he left.

"Got your sermon done for Sunday? Don't forget to plant the Word," John said, realizing he was really enjoying these sessions.

On the way to Cal's church office the next month John was thinking to himself, "I'm beginning to feel like a homiletics professor, I've been giving so much advice to Cal about his preaching." John was a good preacher, more than good, bordering on excellent, by whatever vague measures one might apply to it. He had always been a believer in conscientious and solid preparation for sermons. And during the 1960s and early '70s when there was a lot of talk throughout the church about the decreasing importance and validity of preaching, John stuck to his guns. At pastors' conferences and wherever else he could, he would hold up the importance of good sound preaching. Through the years of his parish ministry he had had numerous interns assigned to him, and he constantly tried to instill in them the importance of giving priority to their preaching.

So he genuinely appreciated Cal's strong interest in becoming a good preacher. His questioning Cal about it was mainly to make sure that Cal would be realistic in his expectations about the results of good preaching. Cal welcomed John into his office with that genuine flash of personality that would be an asset in his ministry. "I brought some fresh croissants from the bakery; I couldn't resist the smell when I walked by," Cal mentioned as he motioned toward a plate full of the baked goods.

"Yeah, that's all I need," John said, "This inner tube around my middle isn't getting any smaller." But he took one anyway. "What's on the docket this morning?"

"Let's talk a bit more about preaching," Cal suggested.

"I kind of thought that was coming; where do you want to start?" John invited.

Cal plunged right in, "What do you think about the whole matter of preaching today? I mean, the church seems to be taking on so much outreach and a wide variety of programs — which are all necessary, I'm not criticizing that — but where does it all leave us in our preaching, in our planting the Word if you will?"

John finished a part of his croissant before answering. "You know, the Word can be planted in many other ways than in preaching. Sometimes, maybe often times, we plant the Word in the things we are doing in the church. Preaching isn't confined to the pulpit."

"I know, and I didn't mean to imply that, but some times ... I don't know ..." Cal's voice trailed off.

John finished Cal's thoughts for him, "You're discovering that there's a lot more to ministry than preaching and calling on people."

"Yeah, there's a lot more," Cal agreed. "Of course, I saw that in my internship year, but then I wasn't the pastor either. He had to monitor all the programs of the church. Now it's on my shoulders."

"And you're wondering if you'll ever have the time to become a great preacher," John teased. "But let's get back to your original question, the one about what I think of preaching in the church today."

"I've heard that you have some rather strong opinions on that," Cal teased right back.

"Well, I won't ask to whom you've been listening. Yes, I do have strong opinions on this subject. I think that preaching has suffered a severe decline in the last 20 to 30 years. For one thing, I think that too many pastors are all too willing to tell people a lot of innocuous stuff, mainly so that no one will get upset with them. In the past 25 years or so I have travelled around the church a lot, and the most frequent complaint I hear from lay people is about poor preaching. My feeling is that people want to hear good solid, biblically-based preaching."

"How many great preachers have you known?" Cal was curious to know.

"I don't know," John began, "There really aren't very many great preachers. And there probably never will be. I'm talking about the spellbinders with the power to hold people's attention like the few great ones of old. In the Lutheran Church there was Franklin Clark Fry. Man, he had a way with words that you wouldn't believe.

"And there were a few others who probably didn't have any national fame or name. Then there were people like Harry Emerson Fosdick who preached at Riverside Church in New York for who knows how long? And in the '30s and '40s there was the great Peter Marshall, who gathered great crowds in Washington, D.C. The only one of these three that I knew was Fry. The others I hadn't heard, but only heard about. And of course I read many sermons by Fosdick and Marshall."

"What about today? Are there any on the horizon?" Cal was still curious.

"Maybe you, who knows?" John teased. Then he got serious again. "But you see, there are never going to be many great preachers, and there don't have to be. I think it is much more important that we pastors be good solid preachers. We don't have to be great, just solid and faithful planters of the Word."

"I think I preach fairly good sermons," Cal ventured. "At least that's what some of my parishioners tell me — but I also want to know what my preaching is producing. Is the planted Word growing?"

John laughed a bit and shook his head. "You young people are really production oriented, aren't you? You know, this isn't an assembly line where you can check off the amount of production at the end of each week or month."

"Well," Cal began rather lamely, "I would like to see some results, some evidence that people are hearing the Word."

"You might be wasting a lot of valuable time looking," John commented, then added, "A long time ago, when I was a young pup in the ministry, an older and much wiser colleague of mine told a bunch of us at a pastors' conference, 'Your task as preachers is to be faithful, not necessarily successful.' That counsel has given me a lot of comfort through the years when I often felt my preaching was not being heard nor acted upon."

"That could sound like it doesn't do a lot of good to preach," Cal suggested, "Maybe like those critics of the '60s you mentioned a few months ago." Cal knew, however, that such was not the case.

And John confirmed it. "No, it's always going to be very important to preach the Word week after week through all your ministry. It's just that you can't be responsible for whether the Word takes root. And an evaluation of your ministry ought not to be made on the basis of how many people have allowed the Word to grow in them."

"How many sermons have you preached in the 40-odd years you've been ordained?" Cal was curious again.

"Oh goodness, I don't know. Certainly more than 52 a year, when you consider all the special services. I suppose I've preached upwards of 3,000. Why?"

"Well, this is kind of crazy, but have you ever considered what effect 3,000 sermons have had on people's lives?" Cal was immediately aware that it appeared he was again looking for a production figure, and that wasn't really what he wanted. "It's kind of a rhetorical question, I guess."

"Yes, it is," John agreed. "Look for a minute at nature. Consider the prodigious amount of seeds that a tree or any other plant puts forth in order that growth might happen. Just take an oak tree for instance. One tree puts out thousands of acorns every year, which is nature's way — or God's way — of making certain that the growth of oak trees continues. Because squirrels and other animals eat most of the acorns, very few of them become new oak trees. Maybe there's a lesson here regarding the number of sermons we need to preach year after year in order to bring forth growth. If we compare the Word of God to those acorns — or any other seeds in God's world — it seems that the Word needs to be preached prodigiously to large numbers of people through the years in order for it to grow in some. Is that too discouraging? It's not meant to be."

"No, I guess it's realistic," Cal admitted.

"Now it's my turn to look at my watch," John commented as he made motions to leave.

"Do you have time to look around before you go?" Cal asked.

"Always got time for that." John remembered the years he had been in the administrative work of the church, and how eager the local pastors were to show him around their facilities. After a brief tour and hearing Cal's ideas on plans he had for his parish, John departed with his usual farewell words, "Plant the Word, Cal, and don't you be too worried about the results — let God do some of the work."

"Thanks. See you next month."

When they met the next month, Cal was a bit subdued. He started their conversation with, "You know, I've been thinking lately that it's a long way from seminary to here."

John asked, "You're not talking about mileage now, are you?"

"No, John," Cal responded with a chuckle. "The seminary could be three miles from here and I would still make that statement."

"Well, it's always been a long way from seminary to the parish, mainly theologically. And you know, part of that is due to the low profile we've had on adult education in our congregations. People are often still in their teenage confirmation years as far as their theology is concerned. That's not their fault ... that's partly our fault as pastors, because we haven't provided enough adult education or haven't given it enough push so that people could become more theologically mature."

Cal observed with some enthusiasm, "But there are some people in my parish who are very alert theologically, and willing to learn. Then again there are others who, as you say, are 'way back in their teenage years.' And then there are some who appear to hear some new ideas or interpretations, but it's mostly surface enthusiasm. And they all hear the same sermons. But I've taken your counsel seriously about continuing to preach the Word to the best of my ability and let the growth take place where it may. At least I'm working on that."

"You'll avoid ulcers if you can remove at least that worry from your mind — that is, about where the seed is going to grow and where it isn't. Of course, you want it to grow in everyone, but even scripture tells us that's not likely to happen." John was pleased with what growth he was beginning to see in Cal.

Cal asked John with a slight tease, "By the way, do you know what the gospel text is for this Sunday?"

John pretended to think about it for a moment, as though he didn't know. "Let's see, is it the Matthew 13 text, about the sower?"

"You got it," Cal responded.

"Been working on it?" John asked.

"Only for about the past nine months," Cal answered. "Thanks to your hermeneutics."

As they departed John gave Cal a gentle hug. "Keep on planting, preacher. Some of those seeds are going to grow."

A Question of Identity

Parallel Parable: Matthew 13:24-30, 36-43
The Weeds Among The Wheat

Ginger Jorgenson was an eager young Lutheran pastor just six years out of seminary. Her first call had been as an assistant pastor in a large midwestern congregation, but for the past year or more she had been in the process of organizing a new Lutheran congregation in rather non-Lutheran territory — in California. The national church body had called her to serve in one of the typical sprawling California suburbs, and she had brought into existence an enthusiastic group of people which was now officially known as St. Andrew Lutheran Church.

"I pushed for that name because I think of St. Andrew as an evangelist," she had told her nearest Lutheran clergy neighbor Lloyd Thompson. "There were lots of weird suggestions for the name of the congregation when we were considering that item," she said, "But I really wanted a more traditional name, something that was scriptural and that had a sense of the evangelical to it."

"We get lots of weird ideas, even in older and more established congregations such as the one I'm serving," Thompson had said at the time.

Lloyd Thompson had been in the ministry more than 30 years when Ginger arrived on the field to start the new congregation. He had made it a point to meet her within days of her arrival, and began what would turn out to be a continuous source of help and encouragement in her work. In addition to helpful advice, he gave her a list of his members who lived in the territory she would be serving. "Call on them," he had advised, "I have told my members that if they live any place close to where you'll be serving, they should seriously consider transferring their membership to the new mission."

She had been pleased and almost overwhelmed by Lloyd's genuine cooperation. He was an old-line mission-minded pastor who wasn't insecure or afraid that a new mission congregation would weaken his own congregation. On the contrary, he had prepared his congregation long before Ginger arrived on the field, to the point that they had set aside several thousand dollars to contribute to the new congregation. Later they took the formal step of voting to have St. Andrew as their mission partner, a program whereby older congregations could give various kinds of assistance to newer congregations until they were well on their way to self support.

But in spite of all the support one might get, there are still rough roads to travel, and Ginger was discovering some of those roads. She made it a point to visit with Lloyd nearly every week, not only to keep him abreast of what was happening, but also to enhance her own experience by soaking up some of his. And she often unloaded some of her parish problems on Lloyd.

"It's almost enough to make me want to start smoking again," Ginger said as she and Lloyd relaxed with coffee and doughnuts.

Lloyd was a bit puzzled. "Well ... I thought everything was peachy keen at your church," he said with just slight exaggeration.

"Oh the big picture is just fine," Ginger responded, "But you know, there are so many weird ideas floating around."

"Right, tell me about it," Lloyd said dryly, "I've been out here for nearly 15 years and it seems that someone still comes up with a new weird idea about every week or so. You gotta get used to it."

Ginger said with a bit of a chuckle, "I guess I thought I could just plow ahead with my own concept of what a Lutheran congregation should be and shape it accordingly. But it's not quite that way."

"Not at all that way," Lloyd said. "I organized a congregation back in Minnesota more than 30 years ago, and I was fresh out of seminary at the time, which was a mistake in itself. But in those days a pastor could set the tone and direction for a new congregation with much more authority than is the case now. And in the procress one could be pretty certain that the new congregation would be solidly and identifiably Lutheran in every respect. Not any more, or so it seems. And I suspect that's true in most denominations."

"Last night we had council meeting," Ginger continued, "and bear in mind so many of these people are relatively new to the church. But it seemed as though I spent half the time trying to ward off stupid ideas and suggestions, at the same time without offending those who suggested them."

" 'Taint easy," Lloyd stated the obvious. "And you know, we always have to bear in mind that the church is made up of human beings, sinful human beings. You and I both know you can't exclude the rascals who are a pain in the butt. We can't create a church where everyone is going to think alike or even be solidly orthodox Lutheran."

Ginger sighed, "Yeah, I know that. Or at least I think I know that. And I don't want our congregation to be exclusive so that it will reach out only to Lutherans. That's not evangelism. I know we need to reach out to the unchurched, and we've done that. My gosh, of the 300 plus baptized members on our charter roll, only about 25 percent were active church members — thanks to you, Lloyd, a good many of those were from your congregation, and they're super people. The rest were unchurched, and we're thankful for that."

"But what are some of the chief concerns you have?" Lloyd wanted to know.

"Oh, I'm not altogether sure I can spell them out," Ginger replied with some hesitation. "I guess sometimes I look back at my home congregation in Minnesota where I grew up. The members were all solid Lutheran folks — or so it seems now. We sang the good solid hymns of our Lutheran tradition, we all knew the liturgy by heart ... I don't know, it seemed we were a more doctrinally cohesive people then."

"Or so it seems in retrospect," Lloyd offered.

"Well, perhaps so," Ginger agreed. "But my first five years in the ministry in Wisconsin were somewhat like my growing up years too."

"Wisconsin and Minnesota are both solid Lutheran country, and you've discovered that California definitely is not," Lloyd said.

"Definitely not!" Ginger agreed again.

"Well, those were the days when we were all Norwegians and Swedes and Germans," Lloyd began.

"In Minnesota it was mostly Norwegians and Swedes," Ginger corrected.

"Okay," Lloyd continued, "But the point is, then we had good solid, predictable Lutheran people. We all believed the same thing — or at least we thought we did. It's a new day now."

"Yes, I know that," Ginger said, "And really, I'm not trying to turn the calendar back. I just want to make sure that we maintain the distinctive character of our Lutheran style of witness as well as our Lutheran identity. We are Lutheran Christians, and we can't be all things to all people."

"Paul said he would be, in order to save some ..." Lloyd started in a whimsical tone.

"Okay, okay," she laughed. "I know that, but Paul also breathed heavy condemnation on many who disagreed with his theology. The Judaizers, for instance, as Paul called them. What would have happened if Paul had succumbed to the very strong move in the early church to make the Gentiles submit to circumcision in order for them to be Christian? Paul said he would be all things to all people, but he set his limits too."

"You got me," Lloyd conceded, "And you're right about Paul. I was needling you a bit there. But what are the limits you think you need to set? For instance ..."

Ginger jumped in, "All right, for instance, we've got a few people who want to teach New Age stuff in Sunday School. Not just as an information course such as one would do in comparative religions, but as an addition to our curriculum!"

"That's a real 'for instance.' " Lloyd conceded again.

Ginger continued, "And we've got the usual folks — many from totally unchurched backgrounds, and certainly from non-liturgical backgrounds — who are bugging the worship committee to kind of ... adulterate, I guess ... the liturgy. I'm sorry, but I strongly believe the Lutheran liturgy is an important part of our identity, and I don't want to see it diluted in order to placate some folks who don't like it."

"I say get tough and kick 'em out!" They both chuckled at Lloyd's facetious suggestion.

"Yes, right, after the way I worked my tail off gathering this diverse group." Ginger sat pensively for a moment. "I guess early on I could have put up a sign that read Only Orthodox Lutherans Need Apply. But not in this day and age."

"Nor in this church," Lloyd added, then asked, "What else? New Age and anti-liturgy. Is that all?"

"I wish it were." She sat again for a while before saying anything further. "You know, this sloppy music some of our folks want to introduce ..."

"Now wait, you are a trained musician as well as a pastor. You can't expect everyone to have your high school musical tastes," Lloyd broke in.

"No, I know that," Ginger said, "And I don't expect that J. S. Bach will be played or sung every Sunday. But this slushy, so-called 'Christian music' that sounds like a tin-horn rock star wrote it ... it's all sentimental slush, like God and I are just pals walking down the street holding hands or whatever. It's bad theology ... and ... and we express and learn our theology partly through our music." She was on a roll.

"I sympathize with you, Ginger, and I agree with you; but — and this may sound strange coming from an old duffer like me — you should be saying this ..."

"Saying what?" Ginger asked.

"That we are indeed in a new age," Lloyd said. "We all might find ourselves having to put up with a lot of things we don't like — if we're to be an all-inclusive church."

"How inclusive are we?" Ginger wanted to know. "I mean, how do we maintain the distinctive nature of the Lutheran witness? Or should we? I believe very strongly that within the Christian fold the Lutheran family has a very positive place."

"I agree, no argument there," Lloyd said.

"Yes, but how far do we allow our Lutheran identity to be weakened and faded by allowing anything to happen and still call ourselves Lutheran Christians? What's Lutheran about us anyway?" Ginger kept pressing.

Lloyd mused, as if chewing on a thought. "I went to a Hispanic Lutheran worship service in the Rio Grande Valley some time ago that you wouldn't have recognized as Lutheran. A mariachi band ... of course, the entire service in Spanish — nothing unLutheran about that I guess ... the hymns were bursting with Latin rhythms and lyrics. The appointed lessons were the same — I think, I couldn't understand much ..."

Ginger responded, "Well, that's all well and good, that's great. But I'm talking about ideas or theology if you will ..."

"And music?" Lloyd teased.

"Yeah, and music," Ginger admitted. "But I don't want our theology, our belief system, to be diluted just to be attractive to everyone. Or even our liturgy. I want us to be inclusive, but not at the price of having to accept every idea people want to plant in us."

"There always has been a tension between being all-inclusive — with all its attendant potential problems — and being too elitist. Look at the church bodies, our individual congregations for that matter, that have tried to strain out everyone except the same orthodox and pure believers. What happens? The most orthodox and pure cadre of those who are left soon find that even some among them are not quite so pure. And so the process of weeding out never ends, and there are split-offs and splinter groups always seeking to be the purest of the pure. All their energies are spent on that pointless enterprise."

"Well, that's certainly not what I'm after ..." Ginger protested.

"Of course not, I realize that," Lloyd interrupted, "I'm just pointing out how difficult it is to know who's in the same boat with us."

"Or field?" Ginger suggested.

"Yes, or field," Lloyd agreed.

Neither spoke for a moment, as though their discussion had about run its course. Ginger sat looking out the window of Lloyd's office, and finally spoke, not necessarily to Lloyd, but rather as though recalling to herself a memory from her youth. "When I was a kid on the farm, my two older brothers and I had a string of chores to do. It just occurred to me now that one of them was pulling up weeds in the summer from our grain fields. I don't know what this particular weed was, but my father called it mustard. It did have a yellow blossom, maybe that's why he called it mustard. But in any case, when there would be an outbreak of it in one of our fields, we could easily spot it because of its color, and we had to hustle out and try to pull it all out. Dad always cautioned us so we wouldn't pull out the barley or wheat or whatever. But that was easy ... we could easily recognize the weeds."

"Harder in the church, isn't it?" Lloyd noted.

"Right," Ginger agreed. "But in spite of all the things we've said about it today, I still get the urge," she said with a wicked growl, "to kick 'em out — that is, everyone except those who think as I do." They both laughed, as Ginger started for the door.

"Don't we all get that urge," Lloyd stated.

"Be kind of boring, wouldn't it?" Ginger smiled.

"You said it, I didn't," Lloyd smiled as they said goodbye.

Role Model Ignored

Parallel Parable: Matthew 18:23-35
The Unforgiving Servant

What is it that leads a person to lie or cheat or steal in order to accumulate more — more of anything? More money, more possessions, more power, more prestige. It is particularly puzzling when a person who is already well compensated for in financial terms and benefits nevertheless has that driving and insatiable hunger for more. What is it about our materialistic-driven world that infects such people? And they are legion, or so it seems. They are found in private business, they are found in government service, and they are found even in the church. Fortunately only a small percentage of the work force are infected. But they're there, and they stick out like a sore thumb when caught in the act.

Some call it sin. Some even call it original sin, against which we all have to brace ourselves. But sin is not a popular concept in the modern world. Most people would rather use euphemisms to describe the condition. So we hear such clever constructs as "strong cravings for power," or "desire to live in the fast lane," or "a web of circumstances he could not escape from." Yes, well, all the decorative coverings we place upon that which afflicts our human family cannot camouflage the truth of the matter: that sin most accurately describes it. Original sin. Born-with-it sin. And it infects all of us, without exception. Like it or not, world, sin is here to stay.

Well, then, what is it about some people who, in spite of the original sin that is in them, can put aside an inclination to seek revenge or punishment upon those who offend them? What is it about some people that they have this strange and unnatural inclination to extend the gentle touch of forgiveness instead of payment due? Why is it that some people can look squarely into the core of an offense perpetrated against them, evaluate it, and decide to neutralize it by deliberately setting it aside, refusing to exact payment or revenge? What is it?

Some call it forgiveness. However, like the term sin, forgiveness is not popular in the modern world. The world calls this sort of thing "being soft," or "naive," or "having a bleeding heart." So the world doesn't much cotton to the concept nor the practice of forgiveness — call it what you will. It's just not prudent, you see. Let someone get away with an offense, and they'll just come back at you with more. No, the practical and prudent thing to do is to hand out punishment that fits the offense. We learned that from the time we were little. The kid down the block hits you, you clobber him right back. Put him in his place. We do that as a nation too. And we break forth with a mighty national cheer when we can bash the enemy, even though they happen also to be God's children. But they brought it on themselves, right?

But forgiveness? I don't know. Too much of this forgiveness stuff and the world would never get straightened out. You've just got to even the score, that's all. So says the world. And the cynics (and some not so cynical) can even point to the Old Testament scriptures to support that kind of vengeful stance. It does say an eye for an eye and a tooth for a tooth, you know.

Vance Erdman was infected, as we all are, with original sin. In him the infection resulted in the insatiable desire to accumulate much more than he needed for a comfortable life. How do you explain that? He was no different from thousands of other people infected with original sin and who will go to any lengths to fulfill their insatiable appetite for possessions. It's quite possible that Vance wasn't even aware of the infection. Like a lot of other people, he learned an intricate system of rationalization to justify his actions.

And for his peace of mind it was quite necessary to rationalize. He was a good solid member of the local Presbyterian Church, the same congregation his boss, Morris Townsend, belonged to. In fact they had served on the vestry together, had attended the men's retreats together. They weren't close friends but they had known each other over a long period of time and shared many of the common interests of other people in their community and in their good solid Presbyterian Church.

But in one or two critical ways, Vance Erdman and Morris Townsend were far apart. And it took about 20 years for the community to discover just how far apart they were. Whatever kind of web was woven by the enticements of the world — whether we call it original sin or something else — Vance was caught in it, as securely as a fly in a spider's web. He had been quietly stealing from Morris for the better part of 20 years. Vance and his family had moved from the hustle and hype of a large city more than 20 years before. They wanted a more peaceful and laid back community in which to raise their children. So they moved without a job and counting on sheer luck to find one. Vance was a skilled accountant. Although he never bothered to get his C.P.A., he was a natural in accounting and figured he might be able to use that skill in getting a job in their new community.

Sheer luck came their way. After attending the local Presbyterian Church for a few Sundays following their move to town, Vance met Morris Townsend, and in the weeks that followed, Morris offered Vance a job at his relatively new company. Just as in the magazine stories of successful businessmen who start a business in their family room or garage, that's exactly how Morris got started with his small manufacturing plant — in his garage. By the time Vance had moved to town the company had grown too large for the garage, and was now in a modest building on the edge of town. Its name was as modest as the owner — The Townsend Company. And keeping books for the fast growing business was proving too much for Morris and his wife and youngest daughter to keep up with. Vance was the answer Morris was looking for to give him some relief.

That was 20 years ago. By now Townsend had built two additional buildings and had a payroll of more than 75 people. But Morris Townsend was still the same gentle man he had been when the business was started in his garage. He held company picnics, and literally knew all the employees and their families by name. He paid them well, gave them excellent benefits and rarely had anyone leave his firm for another job. While he was chairman of the board and president of the company, he was not like big-time CEOs. He was the down-home type, on a first-name basis with most of the employees. And Vance was one of his most trusted.

Still not all was well. Although Morris Townsend was a down-home type of boss, he was not dumb. His business sense told him that the company should have been generating better profits. The company's products were selling well, they were expanding markets every year. And yet the profit was too shallow. Something was wrong.

At a board meeting one month — meetings which Vance attended in order to provide up-to-date financial information — Morris Townsend expressed his uneasiness about the company's profits. He was going to bring in an outside auditing firm to evaluate the company's operations and possibly see where improvement could be made. If anyone had been watching, they might have noticed Vance's jaw muscle working a bit feverishly. And his face might have been just a shade paler than usual.

As well it might have been. The auditing firm sent some of its bright young CPAs to go over Townsend's operations. And it didn't take long for one of the young men to discover that a lot of the company's profits were missing. They brought the information to Morris Townsend privately, and he agreed with their suggestion that they trace the accounting procedures back for several years. Although Vance was certain the auditing firm would soon discover his years of embezzlement from the firm, he cooperated fully with the firm's employees as they probed deeper and deeper into Townsend's books. On the third day they were there, Vance left work early and arrived home before his wife or two teenage children got home.

Vance's wife Betty drove up to their rather affluent looking home shortly after Vance arrived. "Well, this is a surprise, finding you home so early. Are you sick?'' Betty asked, knowing that her hardworking husband was more likely to be late coming home from work than early. In fact, she couldn't recall his ever coming home from work early.

Vance took a few moments before responding. "Well, I'm not sick in the usual sense, or what you might be thinking ..." He paused again, while Betty stared at him with a puzzled look on her face. "But yes, I think maybe I am sick ... or will be ... I don't know."

"But what's wrong, honey? I've never see you like this," Betty asked.

"What's wrong is," Vance groped for words, "that Morris has brought in an outside auditing firm and they're examining all our records going back who knows how many years ..."

"But why is that so bad?" Betty asked a bit apprehensively.

"It's bad because, because, I've been embezzling the old man's money for about a dozen years. That's what's bad." Vance poured it out to his stunned wife in just a few short words.

And she was speechless for a moment. "Honey, did you say you've been embezzling money ... from Morris? How could you when he's been so good to us? You didn't have to do that to provide us with a better standard of living. We'd all be just as happy with a more modest house, and ... and ... well, I just don't understand it at all." She began to cry softly, hoping she hadn't heard him or that maybe it was a nightmare and she'd soon wake up.

Another long silent pause before Vance could answer, revealing even more of himself that she hadn't known before. "It started small, dear," he said in a small, thin voice, as though he was trying to recall just how it all began, just how the crafty web of greed had taken hold of him. "And I didn't take the money in order to provide us with a better standard of living." Another pause. "I gambled most of it away. Most of it I gambled on the horses, but also with bookies on professional sports."

Betty couldn't respond. She was crying and shaking her head, almost as though this was a stranger in her living room, not her husband of more than 20 years. How could she not know that he was a gambler? Was it possible that a person addicted to gambling could hide the fact as skillfully as an alcoholic often hides that addiction? Finally she asked in almost a whisper, "Is that how you bought the kids their cars? I thought you bought them with extra bonuses Morris gave you."

"Yes, those were a couple of things I used the money for, or rather some of the rare winnings I made on the track," Vance replied.

"Chuck's coming up the drive," Betty said in a monotone, as they both heard their teenage son park his Miata convertible near the garage.

"What's for sup . . ." Chuck started to ask, then paused, sensing things were not quite right, and changed his question, "Is this a morgue or what? Did somebody die?"

"No, nobody has died," Vance started to say, but then added, "Yet it's probably worse than a death."

"Well, let's quit playing games, and will someone tell me what's goin' on here?" Chuck persisted.

Vance cleared his throat, then said, "Sit down son. Your father is in big trouble with the company. I misplaced the trust that Mr. Townsend had in me, and through the years I stole a lot of money, probably upwards of a million dollars."

"Oh give me a break," Chuck almost spit out as he got up and spread his arms out in a gesture of not believing what he was hearing. "Is this April fools or what? What gives?"

"A million dollars!?" Betty said, putting her hand over her mouth, "You've gambled that much away over the years?"

"And what's this stuff about gambling, for cryin' out loud?" Chuck wanted to know. "You don't gamble . . . do you?"

"Now just take it easy and I'll try to explain it, although now it doesn't make much sense to me either," Vance began. "I think I must have an addiction to gambling, and years ago I started placing bets on horses or on football games, on anything really. I never won much, and always thought the next time I would win enough to cover my previous losses. And I illegally took money from the company to cover my losses, which apparently got much bigger than I ever thought they would." He paused while Betty and Chuck sat staring into space.

"What's going to happen?" Chuck wanted to know.

Vance pondered that, and finally said, "I don't know what's going to happen. I'll most likely get fired, and I may very well end up in jail ... I don't know."

"Huh," was all Chuck could say, but a wild mixture of thoughts was coursing through his brain.

He was going to say more when younger sister, Mary Beth, came bouncing into the room, fresh from her after-school job at the local Dairy Queen. "How come everyone's so quiet? It's eerie in here," she said as she intended to skip right through the room and get upstairs to her homework.

But Betty said, "Honey, you'd better sit down. Daddy has something to tell you."

"Oh nuts, do we have to listen to the whole thing again?" Chuck said as he made a move to leave the room.

"Now just sit and listen," Betty scolded. "We're all going to have to work on this problem together."

And Vance began to tell the story, in a bit more detail this time. Perhaps the additional telling made it more real or easier to tell, but for some reason he rehearsed the whole sordid tale of his having stolen from the Townsend Company, and would soon have to face his boss and his community and his church — everyone. Lord, what a mess, he thought.

Facing his boss came sooner than he had anticipated. The next morning as Vance came to work at his usual hour, Morris was waiting for him. "Vance, we need to talk," Morris said.

In the privacy of his office, Morris began. "Vance, how much do I need to reveal to you about what the auditing firm has discovered about our company's finances for the past several years?"

"I know the whole story, Morris, because it involves me. As soon as you announced that you were bringing in an outside auditing firm, I knew the truth would come out," Vance began.

"And what is that truth, from the way you see it, Vance?" Morris wanted to hear Vance tell it straight.

"The truth, Morris, is that I embezzled a lot of money from your company over the past several years ... I don't know how many years, and I don't know how much money," Vance began to explain.

Morris said quietly, "The amount of money was upwards of a million — the auditors don't have the exact figure yet — and the time lapse was nearly 15 years."

"All I can say is that I'm sorry, and that I can offer no good reason or excuse for it. And to add to the sordid tale, Morris, I gambled most of it away. Our house and other assets we paid for from my and my wife's earnings. But I know I don't have enough assets to even begin to repay you all that I took. So whatever happens to me, you'll have to decide. And I know I'll deserve firing or a jail sentence or whatever." Vance appeared to be the essence of sincerity as he spoke these words.

"Well, I've thought about it a lot these last few days," Morris responded. "And I've prayed about it a good deal. With my Presbyterian upbringing I have tried to run my business and my personal life according to what scripture tells me."

"I can't argue with that, that's for sure," Vance interjected.

Morris continued, "Vance, I know you can't repay the money, and I don't really expect you to. If you have a problem with gambling, I think that's what you need to address. After a long session of prayer with my wife last evening, I have decided I'm going to write off the debt. Plus I'm not going to fire you nor press charges against you ..."

The verdict by Morris was almost too much for Vance to comprehend all at once. He asked to have the rest of the day off, which Morris granted. As soon as he arrived home, Vance called his wife to announce the good news that had happened to him that morning. Betty was nearly speechless at the news she was hearing. "Why don't you come home for a coffee break?" Vance suggested. "And we'll just discuss it and try to digest the fact."

She did, and they did. "I still can't believe it," Betty said as she sipped at her coffee, "He just forgave the whole thing? But that's just like Morris to do that."

"Yeah, in a way I'm not surprised. It has just taken such a load off my mind — a load that has been building up for years — that I don't know quite what to say or do," Vance commented.

But the euphoria didn't last long. Or rather, it didn't translate into a permanent lesson for Vance. Soon after his wife left for work, Vance dug out from a drawer some of the slips of paper on which he had recorded his latest gambling debts. Most of them were debts that he had owed to the bookies or other gamblers. But he ran across one which indicated that one of his colleagues at work owed Vance a few hundred dollars. "I'm going to call that stinker and get my money back," he thought to himself.

He called his colleague at Townsend. "Ray, this is Vance. I've been going through some papers here at home, and I notice you haven't paid me that money you borrowed at the track a few months ago. I want to cash in this I.O.U."

"Man, do you have to call me at work for that little item? I'm good for it, and I'll pay it as soon as I get a hold on some of my bills. You know I'm good for it," Ray responded.

"The money is overdue, Ray, and I need it to cover some of my bills. I want the money by tomorrow night or I call your wife to let her know you've been gambling again," Vance countered as he hung up.

An hour later, as Ray sat in the company lunch room, he was still angered and in a daze over his conversation with Vance. "What's up, Ray?" one of his buddies asked between bites on a sandwich, "You look like you're in a funk."

"Can you believe this?" Ray responded. "With all the trouble Vance is in with old man Townsend, he calls me and demands I pay him a few hundred bucks I owe him or he's going to go to my wife and tell her I've been gambling again."

"You've got to be kidding," the other replied.

"No, he says 'Pay up or else,' " Ray said, still unbelieving. "With all the mess he's been in here lately, and Morris clearing him of everything, and still he's pulled this ..."

Before the day was out, the word had gotten back to Morris, who reacted with a mixture of sadness and anger. The next morning Vance entered his office as though nothing had happened — either to him or to Morris or to Ray. A note on his desk indicated that Morris wanted to see Vance before he began his day's work.

"Vance, I am sad and I am angry at what I've heard about you and Ray," Morris began.

Vance tried to protest, "Well, he's owed me money for ..." and Morris cut in.

"I really don't want to hear any more from you. I've heard enough. I thought that perhaps my forgiving you your debt to me and to the company would make a changed man out of you, but the lesson went right past you. Pack up your stuff and leave. You are no longer working here. And I'm reconsidering my decisions that I made yesterday."

"So, what's going to happen?" Vance wanted to know.

"I'm not sure what's going to happen," Morris replied. "What I do know for sure is that you didn't learn anything from what did happen. That's the sad part as far as I'm concerned."

As Vance carried his belongings to his car, he still was a bit surprised he'd been fired.

The Contractor's Choice

Parallel Parable: Matthew 20:1-16
The Laborers In The Vineyard

George Gustafson had been a builder in central Texas nearly 40 years. He had come by the trade naturally, for his father having been a cabinet maker and some-time home builder; and even though he was pretty much wiped out during the depression of the '30s, George's father encouraged his only son to pursue a career in the building trades. "People are always going to need a place to live," he told George more than once. George's grandfather had come to central Texas from Sweden just before the turn of the century, and it was from him that both George and his father inherited that inner quality of fine craftsmanship that made them both highly skilled in their trade.

As George's father had been highly respected throughout central Texas for his quality work, George now enjoyed the same reputation in the building industry and to a certain degree among the general public. And George's son Charles, with an engineering degree from Texas A & M, had joined his father's firm and from time to time debated with himself as to whether or not he wanted to take over the business from his father some day. George hoped he would, but didn't say much about it; he would rather have Charles take over because he wanted to, not because Daddy wanted him to.

It was September when George heard from the school board that his bid for the new school building had been accepted by the school board, and could he get started immediately? They needed the new school for classes one year later.

"People who hand out building contracts are all alike," he fussed to Charles (whom he called Charlie). "They deliberate and ponder for weeks, then they give you a contract and say they want the building done on their time schedule. I wonder do they think I'm sittin' on my hands while I'm waiting for them to make up their minds?" George was nearly always an even-tempered man, but he did chafe a bit when he was pressed to get things done in an unreasonable amount of time. And one year to build the new school was unreasonable, considering its size and design, besides the fact that his crews were still busy on other jobs.

"There are contractors who are sitting on their hands waiting for work," Charlie offered, "We're not out of this slump yet, Dad."

"I know, I know," George said rather half-heartedly as he searched the contract for details. "Look at this, Charlie," he said. "They want me to use union labor! I've never used union labor for 40 years, and I'll be damned if I'll start now!"

"Sooner or later — maybe sooner — unions are coming to the south," Charlie remarked.

"Well, they're here, but I'm not using them. They can keep this contract if that provision has to stay in."

"Well, my guess is if they want you badly enough, Dad, they'll give you some room on that," Charlie said, trying to take some of the edge off his dad's reaction to the contract. "You want me to call them and talk about it?"

"No, I know the people there. I'm just going to tell them — as I've told anyone else who will listen — that my workers get better pay and benefits than those of any other construction company, including union employees, and I'm not going to hire union people just because somebody on the school board thinks I should. That's probably what it's about too, some union person on the board insisted that this provision be put in."

Apparently George did indeed get to the right people, because they deleted the union provision from the contract and George began assigning tasks to his key people so the project could get started as soon as possible. "Next September, my eye," he said as he turned the plans over to Charlie and their construction superintendent Tony Contreras.

Tony had been with George for more than 20 years, and he was invaluable to the company. As a Tex-Mex he could communicate well with the Mexican laborers hired from time to time, but he also had a keen eye for analyzing building plans, including spotting errors and goofs made by draftsmen as they drew up the specs. Charlie enjoyed sitting at Tony's elbow in the construction trailer and soaking up some of his experience. "Charlie," Tony said after a long quiet survey of the plans, "It's going to be a job to get this thing ready for turn-key by next September. Maybe next Thanksgiving, but I don't know about September."

"Don't remind Dad," Charlie advised.

"No, we'll just see what we can do," Tony said rather quietly. Charlie trusted Tony's good sense.

They didn't actually get started on construction until the week after Thanksgiving. What with finishing up a few other jobs, getting building permits, arranging for supplies and subcontractors, the weeks simply flew by. They now had nine months to complete the job. Frequent phone calls from school board members wanting to know why the building wasn't up yet didn't help matters.

Shortly after the slab was poured unseasonable rains delayed construction, and patience wore a bit thin. Spring came and went, and George and Tony figured they were about two months behind where they ought to be if they were to be finished by September opening. "No way," George said as they figured what still had to be done.

"Unless ... hmmm ... Tony, I'll tell you what I've been thinking of doing. You and I are going to take a trip into Austin and pick up some of those guys who are hanging around looking for work every day."

"Without knowing what they can do?" Tony asked as though he was hearing things.

"Yeah, there are bound to be a lot of those guys who wore a nail belt at one time or another and could help us out. I've tried the employment agency and I can't get any satisfaction there."

"I don't know," Tony mused, "I'm not sure it's going to work to put guys you know nothing about on our construction site with the crews that know what they're doing."

"Well, look," George said, somewhat in defense, "Maybe we can help this terrible problem of the homeless or the street people or whatever by putting people to work. Hey, if the guys don't work out, we'll drop 'em and try a new bunch the next day."

"Let's go," Tony suggested. He knew better than to try to talk George out of his hair-brained idea.

George and Tony stopped near the Salvation Army building, at the corner where the homeless crowd always gathered looking for a day's work. Some of them wanted work for only one day, enough to buy a bottle of cheap wine and a pack of cigarettes. Others were hoping to land a more permanent job in an effort to get back on their feet. Some had a wife and children whom they had sent to live with relatives in another state until the man found a job. And without a doubt some among them had indeed been fairly good carpenters or masons or sheet rockers before they hit hard times. Maybe George and Tony would be lucky enough to make contact with some of those former tradesmen who wanted more than just a day's work.

George's truck had hardly stopped when it was virtually surrounded by guys wanting work. They knew, as if by instinct, that the truck belonged to a contractor and that the men in the cab had come there looking for workers. These streetwise men had been through this day after day, some of them for years. Some days a few got work, other days a good many of them would be taken away by contractors, and would be back the next morning waiting for the pickup trucks of one or more contractors to pull up at curbside.

As the street people shouted for attention — all of them claiming, of course, that they were skilled workers — the jabbering sounded like an oriental bazaar. Tony was speaking in Spanish to a half dozen Mexicans — who were probably not legally in the country — while George tried his best to pick a half dozen or more men. Obviously, they couldn't take all the guys who wanted to go to the job site, but by some hit-and-miss process, Tony and George together sorted out about

10 men — four Mexicans and the rest an assortment of Anglos — and stacked them in the bed of the pickup.

Charlie was the first person to meet the truck when it arrived at the job site. He suspected that George and Tony had gone to Austin to pick up some workers ... both George and Tony would not have gone off together unless it was for an attempt to get a mixture of Hispanic and Anglo workers. One look at the gang getting out of the pickup bed, and Charlie confirmed his suspicions. Tony gave Charlie a knowing look as he got out of the cab. It seemed to say, "I don't know about your dad ..."

Charlie drew his father aside and asked, "What's the deal, Dad? I kind of thought that's why you and Tony went to Austin, but a whole gang of guys?"

"We need to get that damned school finished, son," George replied somewhat defensively.

"But you don't know anything about them, what they can do, whether they can work or if they'll sit on their butts all day," Charlie said, trying not to sound like he was scolding his Dad. Charlie held his Dad in high regard, but he tightened up every so often when George would do something that seemed a bit too generous or impractical. Charlie knew, for instance, that every so often his Dad would slip a few extra big bills to one or more of his Mexican workers so they could send more money back to the family in Mexico. That was okay, Charlie thought, but this business of getting workers off the street was a bit bizarre.

"Dad, what are you going to pay them?" Charlie asked.

"I told them I would pay them the going rate for the kind of work they can do," George replied, trying to make it sound very logical for his son with an engineering degree. "If they can do the work of a carpenter, I'll pay them carpenters' wages, if they can only do common labor, I'll pay them common labor wages. Now, let's not stand around and talk about it all day, let's get these guys to work. Charlie, you and Tony try to sort out what the guys can do and let's go!"

"They don't have any tools, Dad."

"Well, you know where the toolshed is — come on, get them started."

It didn't work too well. After that first day, George and Tony took six of the 10 back to town — the other four said they would sleep at the construction site that night. The six didn't pan out. They either didn't know diddly about construction work or they were lazy. So early the next morning George and Tony were back in Austin again looking for workers. This time they picked about eight men — and almost selected one of the six who hadn't worked out the day before. After two or three more days of trial and error, they had added a dozen men to their work force, and had found several who had indeed worn a nail belt at one time or another. It wasn't an ideal situation, but they were getting additional work done. Some of the Mexicans they hired had experience in tile work, and were added to the crews that would soon be tiling restrooms and other areas.

But not all was rosy. The regular crew was grumbling. They worked with the newcomers because they had to, but at lunch time they gathered in their own little groups. In fact, the new workers didn't have anyone to pack a lunch for them, so George sent someone to a nearby quick-food stop to pick up sandwiches and soft drinks for the newcomers. That only added irritation to the rest of the crew.

"What's eatin' these guys?" George asked Charlie at lunch time one day.

"Well, Dad, these guys just don't like having a bunch of newcomers off the street come in here and help finish the project. You know, our crew has been out here in the rain and sleet and yucky weather, and now these guys come in in the nice weather to put in their two cents' worth."

"Well, that's just tough. Tell 'em to grow up! I'm responsible for getting this job finished on time, and I'm going to damn well do whatever it takes to finish it!"

"Dad, I'm not arguing with you on that point. I know the job has to be done and I must admit it's working out pretty well now that we finally got some guys from the street who can work," Charlie conceded.

"What's the beef then?" George asked.

"It's the wages," Charlie answered.

"What about the wages?" George asked, although he knew full well that his wage offer to the temporaries would be resented by his regular crew.

Charlie tried to be logical again, "Apparently some of the new guys told the regulars what you offered to pay them, and our guys are just plain teed off. I can't say that I blame them."

"Well, la de da," George replied with some disgust. "Our guys have been fairly treated by me all the time they've been with me. I give them raises and benefits and they've always agreed that they are getting well paid. I still say, what's the beef?"

Charlie then said what he didn't want his Dad to hear, "Our crew thinks it is not fair to pay the newcomers standard wages, when they haven't proven their loyalty. We don't know if we can trust them. We don't know when they'll just take off when we need them most."

"You know what the trouble is?" George asked without waiting for an answer, "They're jealous, that's what. They don't want me to treat the newcomers as well as I treat the regulars; it's as simple as that, and I'm going to tell them so."

Charlie offered some advice, "Dad, go easy on them, they're feeling a bit hurt, and some are a bit angry."

"Well, let's call a meeting for after work today and talk it out," George said with a sigh. "I don't want them stewing about it all during the weekend ... just the regular crew, Charlie, I don't want the temporaries in the meeting."

Charlie and Tony made the rounds during the lunch hour and told the regular crew the boss wanted to meet with them after work. "It's about time," one of them grumbled, hoping neither Charlie nor Tony would hear.

When the crew showed up after 5 p.m. around the construction trailer, the lead carpenter asked in rather hurt tones, "George, how can you pay some of these guys the same wages you pay us, and we've been with you, some of us for several years?"

Another chimed in, "Some of these clods can't lift a shovel ..."

And George broke in, "... and they're getting minimum wage."

"Not all of them," the lead carpenter noted. "A couple of the guys said you were paying them carpenters' scale."

"That's right," George said. "Those fellows who can do the work of a carpenter are getting carpenters' wages. I think that's only fair."

"I think it stinks," one of the carpenters chimed in.

"Well, it's a free country, Sam; you can think whatever you want. But let me ask you, are any of you on my regular crew getting short-changed? Didn't we agree on a new wage scale this year, and am I not paying that?" No one answered, and George didn't expect an answer. He knew — and they knew — they were all getting what they had agreed upon at the beginning of the year.

Since it seemed there was nothing more to talk about, George added, "I'm sure you guys are aware of the fact that if we don't finish this project on time, we get penalized to the tune of $500 a day. Now I would rather have that money go to some extra help so we can get the job done on time than for the money to go back to the school board."

Someone mumbled, "Yeah, he's got a point there."

George concluded the meeting with, "Besides, we're always fussing about homeless people and street people begging for work or for food. So I saw this as a chance to turn some help in that direction, too."

When George returned home that afternoon, after delivering the temporary help back to Austin, his wife Doris asked, "How was your week, honey?"

"Oh, I think we're making some progress."

The Bishop And The Lady

Parallel Passage: Luke 7:36-50
A Sinful Woman Forgiven

"Say, that's quite an enterprise so near to your church," the bishop kidded his host pastor. He was referring to an elegant looking massage parlor just about one block from the church building.

But the pastor didn't think it was all that humorous. "Well, it's technically just far enough from our building to be within the law, but we're not particularly thrilled about its location," he said. "It has been pretty well documented that the establishment does much more than simply offer massages to people. Our members get riled about it from time to time, but there's nothing we can do about it."

"Does it interfere with your worship service ... I mean, is it open on Sunday mornings? Or are your people afraid some of the guys might be patronizing the place?" the bishop asked, again with a bit of kidding tone in his voice.

"Well, no, it's just ... that the place is there, that's all," the pastor replied, just a wee bit defensively. "And the woman who runs the place — she's known all over town as Princess — she even pops into our church now and then ..."

"Maybe she wants your business," the bishop kidded.

"Yeah, right," the pastor quickly replied. "She came into the office a couple times and wanted to give the church some money."

"Did you accept it?" the bishop asked.

"No, not from her, with her reputation," the pastor exuded a bit of piety in that reply. He had picked up his bishop from the airport and they were headed into the parish hall for an informal potluck supper with other pastors from the area.

There was no particular program planned for the evening, just an informal session when local clergy could engage in casual and unplanned discussion with their bishop. He was scheduled to be at an important meeting the following day, but this evening was to be a time of pleasant conviviality with the clergy — part of his "congregation." Bishop Hansen was both popular with the clergy and a bit of an enigma to them; popular because he was always open with them and ready to listen to them. He was a genuine pastoral bishop. But he caused brows to furrow at times because of his viewpoints on social matters. In that regard he was considerably ahead of most parishioners and of even some of the pastors. In his monthly pastoral letter he often took potshots at what he considered false piety.

Princess would not fit the stereotype image of a street prostitute. She was extraordinarily good looking, dressed well but conservatively, and she was gregarious. She liked to be around people. And, oh yes, she owned and operated the massage parlor near the church. And because of the proximity of her business to the church, she did occasionally pop into the church, as the host pastor explained to his bishop. Maybe she just wanted to talk to people she felt were "respectable." Who knows? Maybe she wanted to try for a glimmer of respectability herself.

But she would have to choose this evening to make one of those unwelcome visits to St. Mark's Church down the block. Perhaps business was slow this evening, but whatever the case, Princess noticed the cars and their clergy drivers, and decided to drop in for a pleasant chat with them. And when she did, her eye also quickly spotted Bishop Hansen. The casual dinner had been concluded, and a dozen or so pastors were engaged in conversation, some with each other, others with the bishop. But clergy eyes soon turned toward their bishop and his attentive new acquaintance.

Princess had the bishop's undivided attention for several minutes as they engaged in animated conversation. While no one interrupted, there were some furrowed brows. And whispers. "I wonder if the bishop knows who that gal is?" one pastor asked rather softly to another.

"Do you know?" the other asked with a wry smile on his face.

"Anyone who lives in this area knows about Princess," the first replied, without having to explain any more.

But finally some of the pastors did move over to the bishop, and by ignoring Princess they were able to break up the conversation without being too rude. Princess got the hint and backed off a bit. As she moved toward the door, one of the pastors asked the bishop in a low voice, "Do you know who that woman is?"

"Well," the bishop replied, "I would guess she's the one who runs the massage parlor that Don and I passed just up the block a bit. Yes, she told me who she is, her name is Princess."

Local Pastor Don suggested, "Why don't we get on with our discussion, since Princess has already taken part of the bishop's time? Are there some questions you would like to ask of Bishop Hansen to start things off?"

"Wait. Let's wait a minute before we start the questions," Bishop Hansen requested. "I think we ought to talk about Princess a bit more."

"Was your conversation confidential?" a pastor asked in jest. Everyone, including the bishop, got a laugh out of that, which also served to relax the group.

"No, it wasn't confidential," the bishop replied with a chuckle. "I'm sure she wouldn't mind my telling you word for word of our conversation. I'll tell you one thing, she was one of the most straightforward people I've met in a long time. She wasn't wearing a mask, trying to hide who she was. And her attention to me certainly was not like the attention I often get."

"Which is what?" someone wanted to know.

"Well, let's just say she wasn't trying to butter me up. She was genuine and real. She was who she is, and I appreciated that."

By now Princess had left the room unnoticed. One of the pastors offered, "I would be uncomfortable if she gave me that much attention in front of my congregation — particularly if they knew who she is and what she does for a living."

"Maybe we ought to be uncomfortable from time to time about the people we run into," the bishop responded after a pause. "What is our ministry about anyway? To whom are we speaking with the gospel message? Is the gospel supposed to be reserved mainly for the elite and the respectable and all the folks who have good jobs and wear nice clothes? Is the gospel just for the good old respectable American folks? You all knew the answer to that before I asked the question."

"Well," one pastor offered tentatively. "My congregation is made up mostly of respectable and upright people — am I supposed to apologize for that?"

"No, no," the bishop replied. "You know better than that, Charles. You don't need to apologize for anyone who is in the Body of Christ. Maybe we need to apologize for many who aren't in the Body of Christ. And I don't feel I need to apologize for giving some attention to this woman. As a matter of fact, she gave me 10 one hundred dollar bills — told me she wants it to help feed the hungry."

"And you accepted it, I assume . . ." one pastor inquired.

"Of course I accepted it," the bishop answered — "without apology."

"What's she trying to do, buy her way into heaven? I thought we got rid of that with Martin Luther and the Reformation," another commented.

"Well, now, take it easy you people," Bishop Hansen cautioned. "What is so wrong with her that she becomes the object of your scrutiny and criticism, huh? No doubt we've all read what possibly goes on in some of these massage parlors. And we know there's a lot of extra-marital sex going on elsewhere, too. But we also know what goes on in the board rooms and sales offices and households of alleged respectable people. The financial skulduggery that is motivated by greed, the illicit takeovers of companies so that greedy people can raid the pension funds. Come on, you and I can recite dozens of other illegal and immoral activities that go on right under our noses every day — often by respectable church members."

"True, but that money she gave you still might be tainted," someone offered.

"Could be," the bishop agreed. "But how do you know the source of all the money your congregation receives — in the offering plates? Trace it back two or three sources from your members who gave it, and it might have originated from the mafia or drug dealers. Who can say any money is pure?"

The bishop was on a roll. He continued, "I don't condone what that woman Princess is doing (if in fact she is) any more than the rest of you, but let's look at this a bit more closely. That establishment of hers is allegedly there for the purpose of satisfying one single desire, mostly of men I presume. And we religious people react with disgust and aloofness because of the sin of sexual misbehavior that we think is taking place there. And perhaps rightly so. But what about the multitude of other establishments — different kinds of establishments — that are respectable? The state-sanctioned establishments of lottery all over the country appeal to our sin of greed. Exclusive clubs appeal to our elitism. And on and on you can name them as well as I can."

He paused a bit to let some of his thoughts sink in. He hadn't intended to stretch this discourse out so long, but he wasn't ready to let it drop just yet either. Sometimes the bishop was able to do his best teaching when unplanned events or situations came up, such as the one this evening.

In a more pensive and philosophical mood he added, almost rhetorically, "I wonder why it is that religious people — including Christians — throughout the centuries have been much harsher in their criticism of people who commit sexual sins than those who are guilty of more respectable sins ..."

"Which are ...?" someone asked.

"Which are," the bishop continued, "Greed and avarice and envy and gluttony and pride, to name a few." He chuckled, then asked, "You know, I often wonder if anyone has ever been kicked out of the ministry for being envious ... would any of us have survived?"

"Well, that's stretching a point," someone started to say.

But the bishop wouldn't let go. "No, it's not stretching a point, it's not. Look, the point I'm trying to make is that sin is sin, whether it's the greed of an unscrupulous corporate executive, or ... or .. the activity of this lady — where is she now, did she leave? — who runs the massage parlor? Is her sin any worse than the sin of greed? Or the sin of envy? How many pastors here tonight have been even a tiny bit envious of another pastor who may be serving in a more 'elite' parish? Is she more sinful than that? Or is she more sinful than one who has an excess of pride?"

"I think sexual misbehavior — or sin — is inclined to have more of a social impact than ..." one pastor started to say.

But the bishop headed him off at the pass. "Now wait. The sin of greed that drives a multi-millionaire to take over a corporation and raid its pension fund has a social impact on hundreds and sometimes thousands of people, people who have worked for 30 or 40 years and suddenly have no pension when they retire. That's a social impact. I don't deny the social impact of sexual sins, but that doesn't make it worse than all the rest of the sins that are equally condemned in scripture."

"Well, maybe the sins of that massage parlor, if they are there, are simply more visible to the public," someone conjectured.

"Yes, I guess that's a big part of it, isn't it?" the bishop commented. He continued, "A few months ago I was leading an adult class in one of our congregations and this same kind of question came up. A woman responded in the same way, saying that sins of sexual behavior — whether it be prostitution or some other extra-marital affair — those sins are more public, and therefore they appear to be more serious. And the part that irritates me is that Christians throughout the generations have been quick to condemn those who are guilty of sexual sins — I'm not speaking here of criminal behavior such as rape or abuse which must be condemned — I'm speaking of sexual misbehavior between consenting adults ... where was I? ... we've been quick to condemn those people. But we are often silent about the people within our midst who openly commit sins of greed and pride and envy and gossip, which sins are roundly condemned in Holy Scripture. And I still say, to my knowledge, no one has ever been kicked out of the ministry — defrocked! — for being greedy or envious or proud. Or fat, for that matter!"

"What are you suggesting or concluding from all of this?" one pastor asked.

"Oh, I haven't concluded anything from it," the bishop replied. "I'm just thinking out loud I guess. I think we need to consider sin as sin, and not follow the traditional gradations of sin that places sexual sins in an especially bad category. And as for suggestions, why shouldn't we give some time and attention to the lady who runs this massage parlor? And many others whom we consider to be so 'sinful.' Is she really worse than the rest of us? Maybe she is crying out for attention so that she too can confess her sins and ask for forgiveness."

"And go right on running the massage parlor," the host pastor stated.

"Well, maybe so," the bishop replied. Then after a pause he continued. "You know, I would guess there are people in this congregation who work for the state lottery. The lottery is gambling, and I consider gambling a sin. And those folks who make their living working for the lottery most likely contribute to the church from their earnings. And most likely they attend worship and confess their sins and hear the words of absolution ... and go back on Monday morning working for the lottery, the sanctified gambling operation of the state. Same thing, isn't it?"

Later that evening as the host pastor Don drove his bishop to his motel, they again passed the massage parlor. Bishop Hansen looked towards the establishment and said, "Goodnight, Princess." After a few moments of silence he said, "Maybe she'll show up at your church for worship some Sunday morning."

"Maybe she will," Don replied.

Neighbor To The Man

Parallel Parable: Luke 10:25-37
The Good Samaritan

Minneapolis is a cool city to live in. In more than one sense is it cool. More accurately, in winter it is cold! But in the other three seasons of the year it is comfortable and pleasant. The city is blessed with numerous sparkling lakes within the city limits, plus a generous sprinkling of parks and playgrounds. And churches — particularly Lutheran churches. The heavy accent of Scandinavians in Minneapolis — or at least those of Scandinavian descent — brought forth, early on in the city's history, a plethora of Lutheran congregations, some for the Norwegians, some for Swedes, and even some for Danes. Those of German extraction had their own style of Lutheran congregations as well. Most of those folks came from "the old country" where the Lutheran brand of Christianity prevailed. Hence the large number of Lutheran churches of every brand and stripe.

But Minneapolis has its seedy side also. It has its share of poor neighborhoods and trashy vacant lots — although many of the residents of the city cringe a bit when reminded of that. They would rather think of their city as a clean and upright place. (They would prefer to think of their rival city across the river — St. Paul — as being the seedy place, but then that argument has gone on for years without any noticeable conclusion.)

Henry Daniel had the misfortune on a Saturday afternoon to get acquainted with the seedy side of Minneapolis. Henry was a black man from a small town in Virginia where he taught in a small black college. In Minneapolis for an educators' conference, he had been out for a stroll on Saturday afternoon and got a bit disoriented in some of those confusing streets in what is called southeast Minneapolis. (It's not really as southeast as it sounds — only native Minneapolitans can unravel the confusion.)

As Henry paused beside a weed-filled vacant lot and tried to get his bearings, a car full of white teenage toughs noticed him and stopped to tell him rather bluntly that he was in the "wrong" neighborhood. "I'm attending an educators' conference at the university," he began. "And I guess I got a bit lost in my walk." "Yeah, right," one of the toughs responded. "And I'm the governor's bodyguard." To which his buddies chuckled. Their intent was originally just to give the black man a hard time, but since they each had a few beers in them, the bad time got ugly. And before the toughs sped off in their car, they left Henry unconscious in the vacant lot minus his billfold.

Arvin and Doris Johnson often took a shortcut through this particularly seedy neighborhood on their way to their lake cottage. They were late this weekend getting to their cottage because Arvin had been at his church all morning helping to take care of the large manicured lawn and shrubs. Although he did the volunteer work somewhat willingly, he was a bit irritated this time because he was losing some valuable fishing time at the lake. A mild argument was in progress.

"It was only a sermon, for cryin' out loud," Arvin complained. Once again they were discussing the congregation's participation in the world hunger program, and Doris was hoping to convince her husband that they needed to get serious about aiding in that effort.

"With grandson Jerry newly-confirmed, I'd like to have us set some kind of example," Doris pleaded softly.

Arvin was a life-long Lutheran, as were his parents. Somewhat defensively he said, "Well, I was confirmed too; I learned all that stuff — in Swedish, I might add — and I could still recite some of it in my sleep."

"Reciting it in your sleep doesn't do a whole lot of good, does it?" Doris knew instantly she shouldn't have said that, but she couldn't resist.

Arvin acted as though he hadn't heard. "And you know another thing that ticks me off. All those Viet Nam people or whatever that our churches help to get over here. First thing you know those Asians are going to take over America."

"Well, that's what Jesus tells us we're supposed to do — bring the strangers and aliens in," Doris said quietly.

"Oh, get off the Bible for a change," Arvin said, with some exasperation in his voice. It was difficult to argue these things with his wife because she always had some Bible quotations or other to toss at him. He wasn't sure it was a fair way to argue. "Look at our schools," he continued lamely, "The top of the class is nearly always an Asian — Vietnamese or whatever. And the university here is overrun by all kinds of Asians. Our tax money is going to educate these foreigners!" He was on a roll now.

As they approached the seedy neighborhood shortcut, Doris noticed the black man Henry lying in the weeds. "Arvin, stop! There's a man lying there and he looks like he might be hurt!"

"I'm not going to stop in this neighborhood and probably end up getting hit over the head," Arvin protested. But he was uncomfortable in his protest. "Anyway, he's probably some wino just sleeping off a drunk."

They had slowed down for a stop sign and Doris got a closer look at Henry. "He doesn't look like a wino, Arvin. He's rather well dressed. I think he's been mugged. At least we should stop and call the police."

"Well, I don't see any place to call from, and besides, someone has probably already called the police. Let's keep moving."

They drove in silence until they reached their lake home nearly an hour later. Fishing wasn't all that enjoyable for Arvin, and Doris couldn't get out of her mind the man lying in the weeds.

The Rev. Nikolai Knutsen was eager to get to the seminary. One of America's leading theologians was concluding a series of lectures there, and Pastor Knutsen hadn't been able to hear the first two, so he didn't want to miss this one. He was driving across town to the seminary in St. Paul with his newly-arrived intern, Bonnie Hanson. Knutsen was nearing 40 years in the ministry, and he still wasn't sure he liked the idea of women in the ministry, but that's who the seminary out east assigned to him. He felt a bit self-conscious about it. That wasn't the way it was done in his Danish Lutheran background.

"Where'd you get the name Nikolai?" Bonnie asked in her west Texas twang.

"That's the name of a famous Danish hymnwriter of old," he said proudly, not quite shed of a Danish accent inherited from his Denmark-born parents. "My mother was organist and choir director for a Danish Lutheran congregation in Iowa for many years, and old Nikolai Grundvig was one of her favorites. Unfortunately my voice doesn't do justice to his hymns."

The conversation switched to theology. Bonnie was eager to display her acquaintance with theology, and Nikolai, of course, wanted to demonstrate that he had lost nothing of his theological heritage, absorbed 40 years before in a small Danish Lutheran seminary. As they discussed bits of liberation theology and process theology — both of which were kind of old hat to Bonnie, although seemingly new stuff to Nikolai — they passed the vacant lot where the Johnsons had passed less than two minutes before.

Henry was still down, but not entirely out. His moans had attracted little attention from passersby, most of whom were in cars. Bonnie spotted him first. "Pastor, there's a man lying there!" Whether Nikolai didn't see Henry or didn't want to see, he kept on driving. "Pastor, let's stop and see what's wrong ..."

"Well, I'm not sure there's anything we can do ... I do want to get to the seminary to hear Dr. Marty, and with this traffic...." He was a bit embarrassed and again self-conscious. What could he do? Nothing, he told himself. Besides, someone else will come along soon.

"I'll bet Dr. Marty would prefer that we stop and help this man rather than listen to him, that is, to Dr. Marty," Bonnie ventured.

"Well, I'll tell you what. You seminarians are often a bit idealistic about what should be done and what can be done. We can't save everybody, you know," Nikolai didn't really believe what he was saying, but he kept on driving, mainly because he didn't know what else to do. The lecture at the seminary gave him a feeble excuse, so he pursued it. "It's getting late, and I hate to walk into these things late ..."

They arrived in time for the beginning of the lecture, but neither of them concentrated much on what was being said. And it was a quiet ride back to the church a few hours later — by a different route.

Tran Nguyen and his wife were among those who had recently been brought to America, specifically to Minneapolis, under the sponsorship of Lutheran congregations. As relatively new arrivals, their English was still fractured and limited. Both of them worked full-time jobs — one of them on a day shift, the other a night shift. Plus Tran held down a part-time job. All of which left them little time with each other or with their three small children.

As in the case of so many new arrivals to America, the Nguyens were working toward self sufficiency. They were determined not to be a burden on society, on the country that was good enough to let them in. Their goal of self-sufficiency required ingenuity in scheduling their days and nights, swapping baby-sitting chores with other Vietnamese in their cramped apartment complex. And at this beginning of their life, their supply of money was always short.

Tran was on his way to his part-time job, a job washing dishes in a rather dumpy diner in a seedy section of the city. As his battered, second-hand station wagon stopped for a stop sign, he noticed the black man in the vacant lot struggling to get up. Tran sat stunned, wondering what to do, as people in the cars behind him impatiently honked their horns for him to move on. He did, but something told him to circle the block and check on the struggling man.

In his broken English Tran tried to ask Henry what had happened. Henry mumbled the word "mugged," but the word hadn't yet found a place in Tran's limited English vocabulary. Somewhat urgently he told Henry, "My car ... my car!" Through Tran's grunting English, Henry was able to understand that Tran wanted to take him somewhere. And together they got Henry situated in the front seat of the car.

Tran had taken one of his children to a minor emergency center in the neighborhood a few weeks earlier, and that's where he headed now with Henry and his blood-soaked head. At the center Tran counted out 50 precious dollars — practically all he had to his name — and gave it to the person in charge.

"Wait! Who is this man?" the nurse shouted after the departing Tran.

"I not know," Tran said, pausing in the doorway. "Must go work." And he was gone.

"Who was your friend?" the nurse asked Henry as she dressed his wounds.

"I haven't the faintest idea," Henry replied. "All I know is I got a bit confused while taking a walk, and next thing I knew a bunch of guys jumped me, and when I was partly conscious, there was this Asian fellow trying to get me up."

"It's not a good place to take a walk when you don't know your way around," the nurse offered.

"Well, apparently it was a good place to get some help," Henry smiled through a splitting headache.

Midas

Parallel Parable: Luke 12:13-21
The Rich Fool

The spirit of the 1980's had penetrated far deeper into the life style of Americans than even most economists and sociologists suspected or diagnosed. It was a spiritual disease. The terrible disease AIDS was the numbing physical discovery of the 1980s — a disease that threatened world-wide populations, a devastating physical malady with no cure in sight. But the spiritual malady of the 1980s was as devastating in its way as was AIDS in the physical sense. Especially was this the case in America. The spiritual disease was called greed.

One of the differences between AIDS and greed is that AIDS is a relatively new affliction, whereas greed is as old as dirt, having taken its toll of otherwise well-mannered (and well-intentioned) humans off and on through the centuries. Although it is held somewhat in check from time to time by the sensitivities and teachings of various religions, especially Christianity, occasionally greed breaks out like a ravishing social epidemic. Cleverly disguised and enticingly alluring, it thrives in any culture that holds hard work and free enterprise in high esteem. Especially in America.

Understandably, greed is seldom called by its real name — that would make it too unsophisticated, too taboo. For sophisticated, cultured, civil people scarcely want to use the word greed — it would tend to taint their vocabulary, if not their character, much like the mere mention of AIDS would appear to contaminate their social standing.

Instead it is known by much more sophisticated and acceptable aliases as "taking advantage of the free market economy," or "making a quick buck." Its aliases are legion. They all sound so noble and honorable, no one could ever suspect that greed could be lying close beneath the surface, ready to ravage the conscience and anesthetize the moral principles of any upstanding citizen who might fall prey to it.

But let's call it greed. Ugly, sinful, voracious greed. It is that pernicious and cancerous quality that knows no fulfillment of its appetite. Gently and subtly it can transmutate even the noblest among us into numbing and unfeeling monsters, all the while for seemingly well-intentioned purposes or at least in the process of rewarding people with a sharp eye for opportunity.

America in the 1980s became a swampy breeding ground for the mushroom growth of greed in the human community. Encouraged by a hands-off government which said, "Business will keep watch over itself," plus a host of other talismans, greed grew like poisonous mushrooms. Business flourished. High rollers were the king of the hill. There was no sensible limit to the amount of money any "enterprising" (read greedy) person could make if he/she pulled the right strings, knew the right people, made the appropriate demands at critical moments.

It was called greed. Ugly, sinful, voracious greed. And it infected America in the 1980s in much the same way as AIDS began its deadly infestation of the world. The difference was that we diagnosed AIDS early on in the 1980s, whereas greed went on its devastating path of destruction undiagnosed. Few of those who were infected by greed would have known it and even if they suspected it, would not have admitted it. "Greedy? Who me? No sir!" For respectable people to admit they were greedy would have been akin to admitting catching a venereal disease from a prostitute.

"Greedy? Not me! I'm simply taking advantage of an opportunity."

Greed infected Greg Haldorson in the epidemic of the early 1980s. Raised in a central Minnesota small town, Greg was fed all the usual character-building ingredients typical of rural Minnesota. His hardworking parents were of modest means. Greg learned early the basic value of honesty, thrift, and making money the old-fashioned way — by earning it.

So there was no logical reason for Greg to succumb to greed. He was as willing as anyone else to share with others.

A week at Bible camp in each of three summers confirmed and uplifted the character values he had learned at home. No one would have suspected that Greg would be a victim of greed — least of all Greg himself.

But then no one would have imagined that Greg's uncle would die suddenly, when Greg was in his third year of college. Greg's uncle didn't have any children, and a large chunk of his estate was left to Greg. Two sections of rich farmland suddenly belonged to Greg. He had just turned 21. After his senses recovered, he began to calculate the impact of the gift. It included 1,280 acres of rich farmland — land with a couple small lakes on it — land which could command premium prices at a time when that kind of land was in a seller's market. Without Greg's awareness of it, greed began its intoxicating dance before his fertile imagination.

Greed can (and usually does) cause a variety of uncharacteristic responses in its victims. Greg was not immune to such responses. One response was that he began spending an inordinate amount of time thinking and contemplating what he might do with the hefty amount of money he could get from the sale of his newly-inherited land, if he were to sell to the right parties. He could get money for it. Lots of money. He began reading and studying the *Wall Street Journal* much more than his college texts. And in the *Journal* he kept noticing references to the ripe opportunities for investors in Austin, Texas. In the early 1980s that seemed to be the place where smart investors could put their money, mainly in construction of office buildings. Greg smelled an opportunity to make big bucks quickly. And the greed virus caused him to make a decision. "Go after it," he said.

Instead of hitting the beaches during spring break, Greg returned home to tell his parents he would be dropping out of college after completing his junior year. His parents were stunned. "Drop out of college? What for?" his father asked in disbelief.

Mother added, "You're almost through, son ... just one more year."

"I'm going to sell the land I inherited and turn it over into bigger money," Greg explained.

"But the land will wait until you finish college, Greg," his father pleaded. But knowing Greg, he already knew that his stubborn son had made up his mind. The thing he couldn't begin to understand was why. "Why the hurry, son?"

"I can finish college later," Greg said somewhat uncertainly. "The opportunities for investing in some large projects are not going to be open very long, and I want to get in now while there's time."

"And what kind of opportunities are there that are so urgent, son?" his father asked, "And where — in New York?"

"No, I'm going to move to Austin, Texas, as soon as classes are over. I've been studying investment a lot the last few months, and Austin looks like the hottest place in the country to put some money in the building business. They're building great new offices down there, and you can make big time money putting up some of the seed money for these projects."

Mom and Dad were at a loss for words. They didn't know anything about big-time investment, or any investment for that matter. They knew about working hard for a modest living and being content with what your honest labor could produce. The three of them ate supper that evening under a strange silent cloud. Not much was said of Greg's plans for the remainder of the few days he was home on break. Upon his return to college, he gave only enough time to his classwork to pass finals. He felt he owed it to his folks not to flunk any courses. But even that was a long way down from his usual 3.4 grade point average.

Greg didn't have trouble selling his land for high dollars shortly after classes were over. Developers were quick to pay him handsomely for the land which had such virgin lakeshore property waiting for buyers who wanted to build lakeshore cottages. Greg's move to Austin caused deep sadness in his parents, not simply because he would be removed from them — for they realized that some day he would probably move away anyway. No, they were sad because of the reason for his move. "Where did he ever get infected with that obsession to make so much money?" his mother wondered, to no one in particular.

But Greg was no prodigal son of scripture notoriety. He was careful with his funds, and did thorough investigating before committing any to projects. He had been raised carefully by parents who taught him prudence in financial matters. But he was right. He soon found out there was money to be made in the Austin building boom of the early '80s. No matter that already signs of overbuilding were appearing. As long as building permits were forthcoming, and he had the right projects into which he could put some of his money, he could turn it over fast. And he did.

Three years later, as a young 24-year-old, he was probably the youngest investor in Austin. Not the largest by any means, but surely the youngest, and one of the smartest. He had learned fast. And having the large grub stake from his Minnesota land sale had given him a great start. He wasn't about to call it quits at any time soon.

True to his upbringing Greg worshiped from time to time at a Lutheran church and struck up a friendship with the pastor's son. Tom and Greg enjoyed each other's company. Greg enjoyed being with someone who had no interest in the world of investing or high rolling deals, and Tom was fascinated by this young entrepreneur who resembled a modern day King Midas. "Everything you put your money into seems to turn to gold," Tom said in amazement one night when the two of them sat in a corner of a singles' bar on Sixth Street.

"Well, not everything," Greg pleaded modestly. "I'm making good money, but I'm not wealthy yet."

"Oh give me a break, Greg. You've got that million-dollar estate on Lake Travis, and a condo here in town. What does it take to be wealthy?" Tom smiled in wonderment as he sipped his marguerita.

Greg took his time responding, although Tom wasn't really expecting an answer. "This boom isn't going to last forever, Tom; and I'm going to make the big bucks while it lasts.

In fact, I haven't told you this, but I'm starting to put my money into antiques."

Tom just shook his head. He couldn't understand the drive that made Greg turn his wheels. And he didn't understand that underlying most of Greg's drive for accumulating things was that spiritual disease known as greed. In Austin, as in most of the nation in those years, greed had infected a great many people who had money to invest, as well as quite a few who didn't have any of their own to invest. It was the spiritual disease of the '80s.

"So what are you going to do with the antiques?" Tom wanted to know.

"Do with them? You don't have to do anything with them," Greg answered. "I'm just going to buy them and collect them, because they are precious. They're valuable. And I want them. And do you know that Texas is a great place to get antiques? It's a gold mine out there." He looked across the table at no one in particular, his dreamy eyes seeming to hold in their vision only the prospect of getting some more valuables in his house on the lake.

"I expect that house on Lake Travis is going to hold a lot of antiques," Tom volunteered, not knowing quite where to steer the conversation.

"Oh lordy, that place is nearly full already. I'm thinking I'm going to build an addition onto the house, or maybe another house on the property just to hold my collection." Greg was consumed.

Tom decided to get philosophical. Or maybe theological, he didn't care which. He had been to seminary for a year, and although he decided not to follow in his father's footsteps and become a pastor, his year in seminary caused him to view some things through a theological lens. And this seemed to be a time to use the theological lens, such as it was with him.

"Greg, do you ever contemplate what you're doing with all this moneymaking and purchasing? I mean, where is it all going to lead? What's the point of it?" He was kind of sorry he had asked. He didn't mean to sound like he was preaching, but he wondered if his question had come off like he was.

Greg was slow to respond. "I don't know. I don't give it much thought."

"Well do you know what it looks like to me?" Tom was asking.

"Don't get on my case, okay?" Greg started to say.

"But I'm going to get on your case," Tom broke in. "Because I'm your friend, and I want to see you headed in the right direction. Look, you don't have any social life to speak of. You don't have any women friends, you don't have any prospects for marriage and making a home ..."

"So what? I'm making myself happy ..." Greg's voice trailed off.

"Yeah, right." Tom replied slowly, "I'll bet you are." He paused before starting up again. "You know what I think? I think you're trying to create some kind of heaven here on earth ..."

"Jeez are you getting deep! What turned you into such a philosopher?" Greg wanted to know.

"Okay, okay, so I'm getting into deep water. But let me continue. You're not going to live forever — at least not here in Austin, or on earth for that matter," Tom continued.

"I know, I know," Greg said somewhat apologetically, "I went to Sunday school too, you know."

Tom ignored that. "Have you ever thought who might get all this stuff you are collecting? Your folks surely don't want all that junk you ..."

"It isn't junk, my friend, it's all expensive stuff," Greg defended.

"Call it what you will, but you might be living on borrowed time. We all might be for that matter. And what good is all this stuff if your life comes to a sudden end?" Tom was a bit sorry he had taken the conversation that far.

They sat in silence for a while. Tom changed the subject, "You want to saunter up to the bar and see if we can buy a drink for those two beauties? They don't look like they're spoken for."

"No. You can if you like. You can handle two. I'm going to hang it up for the night. I'm not going to stay at the condo tonight. I've got some things to do at the lake house, and it's already midnight. See ya, when? Tomorrow night?" And Greg left, followed soon thereafter by Tom.

The next morning, as Tom gave a quick glance at the morning paper, his mind froze. The headline read, "Jaguar Misses Curve on 2222, Local Developer Dead." Tom cried all the way to work.

I've Heard That Song Before

Parallel Parable: Luke 14:16-24
The Great Dinner

"I suppose you're aware of the fact that Uncle Henry's annual bash is coming up soon," Chad said to his cousin Will. The two cousins in their mid-30s were trying to get a quick nine holes of golf in after work while there was still enough light to see the ball.

"It seems to me I've heard that song before ..." Will responded, half singing, half humming an old tune from the '40s.

"Where'd you dredge up that old number?" Chad asked as he pitched his shot toward the green.

"From Uncle Henry, where else? He loves those old songs — 'When they had real music,' as he says," Will replied with no intent to criticize their uncle.

Chad continued about the annual affair, "Well, it's probably going to be the same old song and dance. He puts on the dog every year, invites all the bigwigs in town. Plus all the relatives."

"You could have left that last part off ..." Will started to say.

"Yeah, well, we gotta go, because we're part of the family ... and ..." Chad began.

"And if we don't, we might get cut out of the will — is that what you were going to say?" Will teased.

"Hey, gimme a break ... hell, now I missed that tap-in putt. See, you had me thinking about old Unc Henry and not about my putting stroke," Chad chided his cousin.

"Right, blame me for your putting ..." Will defended.

"No, I'm not blaming you for my funky putting stroke, I'm blaming you for carrying on so about Uncle Henry ..." Chad responded.

"Hey, you brought it up," Will countered. "But I guess it's on all our minds these days. Can't avoid the subject. Ole' Unc Henry and his idea of a party. He can't get out of the 1940s, back in Pennsylvania."

"Well, when the money comes rolling in from his will some day, you won't care if it's 1940 or 1990 money!" Chad said with a smile.

"Yeah, if I'm in his will," Will said with just a touch of doubt.

"Oh, you can't miss — especially if you come to his party. You know he likes to parade his relatives before the townsfolk," Chad reminded him.

Will paused while he hit his drive, then he sighed, "Right, the party. Damn!"

Henry did have a lot of kinfolk in town and in the surrounding counties. But he was also known as "uncle" to a lot more people than just his family. He was a semi-retired super successful business entrepreneur, a wheeler-dealer in a town that had grown through the years into a small city. And though he had lost none of his power and influence, his annual party was getting a bit dull to some folks.

Henry's wife had died nearly 30 years before — after they had been married 20 years — and every year since her death he threw a party to honor her birthdate. They had no children, and he had never re-married. After his death Henry devoted most of his waking hours to his various business enterprises. In addition he spent a large share of his time in community improvement, and in serving his church. So he had a high profile in the community and was known by hundreds of people.

Truth be known, Henry was somewhat eccentric, no doubt about it. Always had been. He fit the common stereotype of an eccentric wealthy man who wielded power and influence even when he wasn't trying. His power and influence stemmed mostly from the common knowledge that he was wealthy, and people knew what he could do with his money. His eccentric nature often caused unpredictable swings in his mood as well as in his plans and actions. Hence there was a significant group of people who nervously watched him in his every mood swing. Those who were particularly nervous were people who might some day be recipients of his largesse.

Such recipients included his relatives. Although he had no children, he had swarms of nieces and nephews, all of whom received unexpected gifts from time to time — depending upon how sensitive they had been to his need for attention. Most of his nieces and nephews were now young to mid-30 adults. When they were children they sensed that if they visited Uncle Henry frequently, they might be rewarded with a new bicycle or something equally attractive. But as they got older they realized that the one thing Uncle Henry wanted from them — as well as from the important movers and shakers in town — was their presence at his annual bash. He wanted to show them off.

Uncle Henry still loved his long-departed wife. The annual extravaganza was his way of letting everyone know that his love for and loyalty to her had not diminished through the years. Of course, he usually used the occasion also to wax eloquently on his favorite political discourses, and on everything else on which he had abundant opinions. And when all the invited guests showed up, including the somewhat spoiled relatives, it was an exclamation point of his statement of dedication to his departed wife.

But as time passed, nearly everyone had forgotten what the original reason was for the great outdoor party. They came for a number of reasons: partly because of the extravagant provisions, partly because all the "important" people would be there, but mostly because they realized Uncle Henry would know of any who didn't show up. He kept a mental tally as he strolled through the grounds of his well-manicured place, and under the gigantic tent that was brought in each year for the occasion.

Yet in spite of its long tradition, the annual party was losing part of its charm. Maybe it was the town itself, now that it had outgrown its coziness and had become a small and vibrant city. With all the growing business and civic activities taking up more and more of people's time, there were other functions to attend. And there were other parties. Parties where one could find more influential people than would be at Uncle Henry's. These new galas were now the kind of attraction that Uncle Henry's were 20 years ago.

So it became more and more of a chore to get excited about Uncle Henry's annual affair. His live replica of a big band playing swing music of the '40s simply didn't turn on the new crowd. And his nieces and nephews couldn't stand it.

"So how are you going to get out of the party?" Chad challenged as they walked down the fairway.

"I don't know," Will said with no enthusiasm. "Maybe I'll get sick. What about you?"

"I think I have a business trip coming up which I can't avoid," Chad answered in pretended seriousness.

"You're rotten to the core, you know," Will chastised.

"Can I help it if business demands so much of my time?" Chad replied with a knowing wink. "Your sickness excuse won't hold water you know."

"I know," Will agreed. "What's the date of this thing?"

"Right smack in the middle of May — May 15, I think," Chad guessed.

"You're kidding!" Will said with an enthusiastic start.

"No, why?" Chad wanted to know.

"I'm in a wedding on the 15th!" Will gleefully shouted.

"Not another one of yours, is it?" Chad teased.

"No, smart alec," Will answered without defense. "An old frat brother — he was in my first wedding — or was it my second, I don't remember. But who cares? I've got a wedding to go to!"

"Well, there goes your name out of the will," Chad said casually.

"No way, cousin. The old guy's sentimental. When I tell him I have to be in an old buddy's wedding, he'll understand. It's a done deal. And, by the way, is your business trip for real?" Will tried to get the last word in on the best excuse to come up with.

"I'll make it for real," Chad said with some determination. "Of course, it was supposed to be a week later, but for some reason or other, I'll have to move it up ..."

"Yeah, right. I knew you were rotten, cousin," Will said as they both chuckled at the convenience of their schedules.

Uncle Henry sat alone in his walnut-panelled study going over his mail and telephone messages. It used to be that anyone who was anyone in town would wait to set their spring calendar until they heard from Uncle Henry about his annual party. Then they would work their schedule around that important date. Not any more. The party had lost some of its glimmer, and now played second fiddle to almost anything else. Henry was still important in the community, but his party was not. As he sat looking at the mounting pile of polite notes and phone messages, he shook his head. He wasn't so much angry as bewildered. "I don't get it," he thought to himself. "For years everyone came to my annual party to honor Helen. This year they've all got other things to do."

That wasn't quite accurate. Not everyone declined his invitation. But the number who did was too many for Uncle Henry. He was particularly upset about the number of relatives who couldn't make it to the party. "I don't get it," he repeated. "Even my nieces and nephews can't come. High school graduations, weddings, business trips ... who knows what else ...?" Even the mayor had sent his regrets. A major political meeting was to be in town that very weekend, and he couldn't possibly be absent from such meetings.

He paused in his pondering. Then his old eccentric brain sparked an idea. "Damn!" he said as he practically ran to the kitchen where George, one of his long time employees, was making initial preparations for the lawn party. "Ain't no one gonna stop ole' Henry from havin' his annual bash," he shouted as he spotted George.

George looked up without any sense of surprise, long since accustomed to Henry's eccentric ways. "Mr. Henry," as George always called him, "You look like you got fire in your eyes." Wise old George knew something was afoot.

"George, don't cut back on any of the preparations for this year's party ..." Henry started to say.

George cut in, "But I thought the crowd would be 'way down this year, Mr. Hen ..."

But Henry interrupted, "No, George, it might very well be much larger. We'll make it the best year ever!"

"Yes, sir," George replied, wondering what might be up this time.

The city's one newspaper always reported on Henry's annual party, in the society section, of course. But this year it was reported on the lower half of the front page. The story began:

> "Hundreds of people gathered once again for the annual party known for years as 'Uncle Henry's Bash.' As usual, food and drink aplenty were available on tables scattered throughout Henry's well-manicured place. The unusual part of this year's party was the guest list. Missing from the party were such city movers and shakers as the mayor and several of Henry's relatives. Seems as though too many conflicting events were on the calendars of the usual guest list. But the party was crowded to overflowing nonetheless. And here's the kicker: Henry had hired taxis and limos to bring several hundred street people and homeless folk to the party! 'Best party I ever had!' a smiling Henry said as he strolled over the grounds greeting the homeless."

Which Ones Were Lost?

Parallel Parable: Luke 15:1-10
The Lost Sheep, Coins

The first time I set eyes on that grand old church building was in the cool of a January evening. Since it was in a southern state, there was no chilling cold to make me hurry back into my host's car, so the two of us casually made our way around the empty building. He was a synod president, and I was a churchwide senior staff person on an official visit to his synod.

The beautiful old building was locked tighter than a drum. There were quite obviously no meetings taking place in it that evening, which my host regretted because he was eager to show me the inside of the church. "No problem," I said. I had gotten into enough locked churches before with my trusty pocket knife, and with a few twists of the blade on a kitchen door latch we were inside the building. The fast-fading twilight was just enough to fire up the beautiful stained glass windows of the sanctuary and give us a picture of the worship area. Actually the sanctuary, both inside and outside, appeared to be much older than its 22 years, as indicated on the cornerstone. But new or old, the interior gave an immediate feeling that this would be an inviting setting to worship. The silent invitation of the sanctuary and chancel would appeal to one's need for private meditation or to a stirring Sunday morning celebration — take your pick.

As we left the church and began the short trip to my motel, my host casually noted (at least he thought it was casual), "The pastor of this congregation will be retiring in a year or two."

"So?" I responded, trying to sound neutral, although I suspected what he was digging around for.

"Would you have any interest in having your name submitted to this congregation when the time comes that they are looking for a new pastor?" Might as well put it right on the line, he must have reasoned.

I gave the response I had given to others when that type of question had been asked of me. "I don't know. I know nothing about the congregation, and I don't know where I'll be or what my learning might be whenever this congregation's present pastor retires." In retrospect I have to admit that wasn't entirely straight. In those brief moments just walking around in that half-darkened church I had the strange feeling that this might be the place where I would be serving some day. Weird. Sure I was in some strange way interested. But in those days it wasn't polite to say so. So I gave my standard response. I was polite.

Three years later I was back in that church, this time conducting Sunday morning worship. Following the worship service I met with the church council to talk about housing and other matters. A few months prior the congregation had issued me a call to become their pastor. After scurrying around town and fortunately finding a good rental house near the church, I was able to be alone in the sanctuary in the cool of that Sunday evening. And I recalled being there three years earlier. Somehow I felt at home. This was my place to be. I knew I would be enjoying my ministry in this place and among these people.

A few months later our family moved to our new southern location. I began my ministry there with a flurry of activity — meeting members, attending meetings, getting programs propped up. Yes, I was enjoying my ministry there, and it was indeed good to return to parish services. A bonus factor was the beautiful old-looking church building with its worship-inviting sanctuary.

But I was bothered by the church doors being locked, locked 24 hours of every day except Sunday for a few hours in the morning. It was like a museum. A beautiful museum no doubt, but people could see it only on Sunday morning. Since it was located near the university, there was some pedestrian and considerable auto traffic past the church. "What if some of those passersby want to see the inside of the church?" I had asked myself. "Or what if some troubled student or other person wants a quiet place just to sit and meditate?"

So prior to my first formal meeting with the church council I put together a logically reasoned proposal. It was to leave the church doors open from dawn to darkness seven days a week. Not just unlocked, but standing open. I explained to the council that I wanted people to be able to walk in and sit in this beautiful sanctuary, to pray if they wanted, or just to meditate and be quiet, away from the hurry and hustle of the streets.

They had been without a pastor for nearly 10 months, and were so glad to get someone on board full-time that I guess I could have asked for — and gotten — anything just then. The council thought it was a good idea and unanimously passed the proposal. Interior doors were to be secured in such a way that people coming in could not pass from the sanctuary to other parts of the building, in case some might have had intents other than praying. That satisfied any uneasiness council members might have had. So starting the next morning the exterior doors were opened from dawn to darkness every day. And all were happy.

But not ever after. For this was also the period in our history that the hippie movement was in full swing. And the church building, located near the university, was also in the pathway of numerous hippies. Some were just wandering about, with guitars slung over their shoulders, maybe a bottle of cheap wine with them. Others were on their way to one of the parks across the street or a few blocks away probably looking for a secluded spot where they might smoke a joint.

It wasn't long before hippies discovered that the sanctuary of the church, with its open doors silently inviting people to come in, was a cool place to be. And so they came in. Not often, but every week one would notice one or more hippies going in and out of the sanctuary. From time to time when I went into the sanctuary for one reason or another I would spot a few of the flower children sitting on the chancel steps. They might be strumming a guitar and humming a tune. Or they might try to hide the bottle of Apple Ripple they had brought in with them. But they did no harm. Ever. They found the sanctuary to be just that — a sanctuary from the busy and commercial world about them. Would that the busy men and women who were not hippies would have taken a few moments each day or each week to step into the sanctuary for that same reason! I often stopped to chat with them and eventually got to know several of them by name.

But you see, the hippies weren't like the rest of us. They dressed in weird, non-conventional ways, they lived in groups in ramshackle rental houses. And some people thought they needed to bathe more frequently. I don't know, I don't recall smelling any of them. But there is no doubt that the hippies were not well received by the general populace. They protested a variety of things that went on in society. They gathered in their hippie hangouts all over town. They smoked pot. And in general they were a sore embarrassment to the straight "decent" folks. Hence when some of them frequented our open church sanctuary, some of our people were upset. The upset folks were only a small minority, but they made much noise about it. More than one person came to my office to complain about it.

"But they're not doing any harm to the building nor to people," I reasoned. But my reasoning often fell on deaf ears.

"Tell them if they clean up and wear decent clothes they will be welcome in our church." That line was often used by the vocal few who objected to the hippies' presence.

Again I protested, "But do we now have dress codes for people to come into our church?" Again my protest fell on deaf ears.

It was a standoff. I kept referring to the fact that the church council had, a few years earlier, adopted the policy of open doors with no restrictions on who could or could not enter the building, and I intended to defend that policy. Of course. I was the one who proposed it. And as the months passed, we saw signs that some people were indeed often using the building for prayer and quiet time. As evidence of this, we collected the thank you notes that people had written and left in the pews, notes that expressed appreciation that the church sanctuary was open when some person was in need of a place to think or pray.

And then there was the rose on the altar. One week I noticed a solitary rose lying on the altar, placed there by an anonymous person. The rose was accompanied by a note which promised that a fresh rose would be placed on the altar each week until the conclusion of the war in Viet Nam. And for many months thereafter we became accustomed to finding a fresh rose on the altar each week although we never did discover its thoughtful and sensitive donor.

But the subtle benefits many of us saw in having the church doors open were missed by the few who opposed the policy. From time to time when some members of our altar committee would go during the week to prepare the altar for Sunday worship, they would be upset by the sight of a few hippies sitting on the chancel steps. Were any of our people ever in danger or threatened? No, they simply didn't feel comfortable with hippies in their midst. And they wanted something done about it. Maybe call a congregational meeting. But instead we held an open forum to discuss the whole matter. After a long evening little was resolved except to reaffirm the policy of leaving the doors open for anyone who wanted to enter.

As time passed and I became acquainted with more of the hippies, I was told at times they were in need of pastoral services, such as when one of them died from an overdose of drugs. Would I conduct a memorial service for the person, they asked? Yes, I would. And did on several occasions. In addition I performed the wedding for several hippie couples, on those infrequent occasions when two of them decided to formalize a relationship that had been in progress for quite some time. And from time to time I dropped in on some of the hippie hangouts just to shoot the breeze.

Such contacts would not have gone unnoticed, particularly by the few in our midst who were most critical of such associations. Those few asked me to meet with them to discuss their concerns. What were their concerns? Mostly the people I associated with from time to time. "You can't save everybody, pastor," one of them observed. "Some people are going to be damned no matter what you do, so take care of those of us who have not strayed from the fold."

"But didn't Jesus say that we must seek those who have strayed from the fold?" I asked, somewhat innocently. "Didn't Jesus imply that it was okay to leave the 90 and nine who were safe and go into the wilderness to search for the lost? I think that's the church's main task."

I was sad. Not because these few people had raised such vociferous objections to the whole hippie question, but sad because I wasn't getting through to them. I was sad because those few folks apparently wanted their church to be untainted by unwelcome people. And they wanted their pastor likewise to be untainted. I was tempted to appease them by assuring them, "You people are among the 99 who are saved. You're not the lost ones who need to be found."

But as I reflected on it later, I wondered which ones were the lost? I didn't want to make a judgment on it, but I wondered just who were the lost? Were the lost sheep those harmless hippies who gathered in their groups and smoked pot and sang their songs about the lostness of the establishment? Were they really lost?

Were they lost because they protested many of the tightly held values of the vast majority — the people they called the establishment? Were they lost because they protested the war in Viet Nam? Or because they protested killing fellow human beings, no matter who those human beings were or what country they belonged to? The irony in all this was that most of the hippies took seriously what we had taught them when they were children in Sunday school. We had told them that it was wrong to hurt people, and particularly that it was wrong to kill other people. And they took us seriously! They believed what we had taught them in Sunday school! So now, when they were adults, or in some cases almost adults, they said it was wrong to kill people. And we criticized them for saying so, particularly because our country was officially killing thousands of Asians — and in the process sacrificing thousands of our people. The hippies said it was all wrong.

And when they sat in our beautiful stained glass church on week days and sang their sad songs, some of our people were upset. "The tax collectors and sinners were coming near ..." Luke tells us in his gospel. And he continued, "And the Pharisees and the scribes were grumbling and saying, 'This fellow welcomes sinners and eats with them.' "

Perhaps the saddest part of the story is that there is often no clear definition of who is lost. Really lost. The scribes and Pharisees in Jesus' day definitely didn't think they were lost. No way. They had upheld all the traditions and laws of their fathers and of Moses. And in the late 1960s those who despised the hippies, or were upset at their invasion of our sacred place, didn't think they were lost. They had been faithful church members all their lives. They didn't protest against the establishment. They didn't smoke pot, and they wore decent clothes. And they bathed regularly. How could they be lost?

And in a sense they were right. But I often wondered, "Which ones were lost? Really lost?"

A Woman Had
Two Daughters . . .

Parallel Parable: Luke 15:11-32
The Prodigal Son

Erick Nielson became acquainted firsthand with the Great Depression of the 1930s on a farm in North Dakota, not far from the state's largest city, Fargo. Even as the state's largest metropolis, Fargo wasn't all that large in the '30s, probably with a population of not more than 30,000. But it was the center of a large sprawling farm population where farmers for miles around brought their produce and did their serious shopping.

The Nielson family — like many others — didn't do a great deal of shopping in the '30s, mainly because there wasn't much money with which to shop. But they brought their cream and eggs and butter to the creamery in exchange for a small amount of cash. But the cash crops brought so little money that the family finally decided in the mid-'30s to give up farming and move to Fargo. Erick's father found a variety of jobs to keep the family alive, and when Erick had graduated from Fargo's only high school, Central High, he was lucky enough or plucky enough to get a job with a farm implement company. His pay was $20 a week, and it stayed that way for more than two years. But he learned about the farm implement business, which would prove to be an asset in those difficult times.

Eventually Erick was drafted to fight in World War II, but when he returned, he not only returned to the farm implement company, but was soon made manager. The Depression was over and there was a positive fallout from those scrimpy times, a fallout that was etched in every fiber of Erick's character: the value of working hard and of keeping a close watch on the dollar. In short, he learned frugality. And in a few years his hardworking character enabled him to buy into the company. Before too long he was sole owner. And though by now the Depression was long since over, and his financial situation had vastly improved, he continued the same frugal money management in his home as in his business. To this good Catholic it was simply good stewardship of whatever came to him by God's grace — or by his hard work — to take good care of his possessions.

Meanwhile he married Mildred Carlson, whom he had met in high school. His prudence and frugality, spawned in the Depression, told him early on in his marriage — and after first daughter Erica was born — to set up a fund for any children he and Mildred might have. The fund was loosely structured, its main provision being that the appropriate child could begin withdrawing it at age 18, whether its intended use was for college education or any other useful purpose. For eight years Erica was an only child, then second daughter Estelle came along. Her father immediately set up a separate fund for her use when she would turn 18.

After a few years it became evident to the family and friends that the two daughters were no two peas in the pod — not by any stretch of the imagination. Somehow the mystery of genetic distribution had given older daughter Erica many of the noticeable and admirable characteristics of her father. Even as a pre-teen, she displayed those solid work ethic principles of hard work and determination to contribute her share of responsibility to the community. Except for her gender, she was made in the image of her father. Perhaps it was no accident that her name was the female form of Erick. She never gave the folks much trouble, she excelled in her school work, and made plans early on to enter the University of North Dakota 70 miles north in Grand Forks.

But Estelle was another story. From the time she could walk and talk she seemed to exude a rebellious spirit. She showed a fire and a zest for life that later might be interpreted as a lust for life. In the heart of her spirit was an intense fire, banked like that in an old fashioned furnace. Whatever alchemy of genes from generations back had produced this deep and mysterious daughter eluded the understanding of both Erick and Mildred. Her mother often pondered quietly the differences between her two daughters, almost as though they were from two different sets of parents. And strangely enough, father Erick rather secretly twinkled with delight at this frisky young daughter who seemed not to fit into any pre-cast mold. He often repeated that old standard bromide, "They sure tore up the pattern after she was conceived."

Partly because of their age difference, the two sisters never became close pals. Erica — even at the tender age of 12 — often acted like a stern aunt to four-year-old Estelle. And through the years she watched her growing up, perhaps secretly wishing she had the capacity — or the will — to treat life as one grand party, as Estelle already seemed to be doing. That somewhat odd and aloof relationship would continue long past the adolescence of them both.

Erick didn't help matters much by the way he doted on Estelle, to the point that he often overlooked many of her pranks and escapades as she quickly zoomed from little girl to pre-teen. But suddenly Estelle was left floundering, not yet grown up, when her father was stricken with a heart attack and died before he could be taken to a hospital. Erick's untimely death was devastating not only to Estelle, but also to Mildred and Erica. Mildred had worked off and on in her husband's business, and she knew — without the question even being raised — that she was going to step in and run the farm implement business Erick had worked so hard to build up.

Erica was in the middle of her junior year at the university, but instinctively she knew she would be needed at home to help her mother run the business. She returned to Grand Forks after the funeral to finish her semester exams, but then was back in Fargo.

Her major in business would be put to immediate use. So after the chrysanthemums from the funeral had been re-planted in the yard, and all the thank-you notes had been sent, the hard work was about to begin. Mildred and Erica were determined that the business would go full speed ahead.

But there was also the matter of Estelle, a wide-eyed 12-year-old who now had lost her bearings with her doting father gone. Mildred gave her as much attention as she could spare from running the business, but it wasn't much, perhaps not enough. Anyway it was a bit forced, since Estelle had always received more than enough attention from her father. So Estelle gave herself attention. She buried herself in books — not necessarily school textbooks. She coasted through high school with no particular goal in mind in the event she should finish. Yet finish she did, but college was not in her sights just now.

Nor was the family business. No, she wasn't enamored with Fargo nor of the farmers who tended the rich flat land in the Red River valley. She wanted out. So when she turned 18 a few months after graduating from the Catholic high school, she made a startling announcement at the dinner table, at the end of a day when both mother and sister had been particularly overworked — and still had to prepare the evening meal.

"I would like to withdraw the money from my trust fund, Momma — all of it," she announced rather tentatively. She wasn't too concerned what her mother would say, but she knew her sister would once again act the role of stern maiden aunt. She was right.

Good down-to-earth Erica asked incredulously, "What in the world do you want with it all at once? That's supposed to be for more than four years of college."

"I'm not going to college," Estelle stated, as though that would already have been assumed by her sister and mother.

Erica sat back in her chair and rolled her eyes, trying once again to make sense of her younger sister. "What are you going to do with all that money? Just carry it around in your jeans?"

"I'm leaving Fargo for one thing," Estelle said, again in a tone that suggested this announcement should not surprise either her sister or her mother. "I'm outa here, as soon as I can get my grub stake."

"Yeah, some grub stake!" Erica spit out the words. "You'll probably blow it in no time and have nothing to show for it. And how are you going to take care of yourself? You don't even know how to fry an egg!"

For her part, and to her credit, Erica had finally completed her college degree, squeezing in courses when she could break away from the business. But it took her all of the six years since their father died, to get her degree. And Erica, prudent Erica, managed to do so with the majority of her fund still intact. Hence her apprehension and concern at Estelle's crazy request to withdraw all the money that was in her fund.

And mother Mildred didn't object. Actually there was no point in objecting. Each fund was set up with the only restriction being that each daughter must attain the age of 18 before beginning to withdraw the money. So Mildred said, in quiet resignation, "Well, if that's what you want . . . ."

But before she could finish, Erica interrupted, "Oh yes, just fine! 'If that's what you want!' You seem to have taken up where Dad left off six years ago. That's what he always said when this spoiled brat wanted anything — 'If that's what you want.' " She angrily left the room before any response was forthcoming from either Estelle or Mildred.

A few quiet moments after Erica stormed out Estelle observed dryly, "She's sure in a friendly mood tonight."

"Now get off her case," Mildred scolded mildly. "She's been carrying a heavy load in the business. And I notice you haven't even walked into the place for months."

"Farmers and farm implements aren't in my horoscope, Momma. How soon can I get my money?"

"This week, if you want it that soon."

"I want it that soon." And she got it, the whole nine yards, which she quickly converted into cash and traveller's checks. It was a satchel full.

Within a week she was gone. Before she left, her mother had asked her in some frustration, "Do you know where you're going or what you are going to do?"

"Momma, I really don't know," Estelle had answered impatiently. "All I do know is that I'm getting out of this cold, windy farmers' market called Fargo! I'll keep in touch." The fire within her had not diminished through the years, but instead seemed to inflame her spirit more intensely. It was not to cool down for a few more years. Before she left, Estelle had popped into the family business and said a quick farewell to sister Erica. There was no visible emotion in their parting. "I'll keep in touch," Estelle promised half-heartedly.

"Right," Erica responded, not for a moment believing her sister.

And she was gone.

An airline flight took her to Minneapolis where she stayed with a friend for a month, meanwhile meeting a bunch of new friends — or at least exciting and fun companions. From there she and a new friend — improbably named Lolita — flew to Chicago, at Estelle's expense, where Lolita had numerous contacts. It was the exhilarating and exciting life Estelle had envisioned for the past few years. For weeks she and Lolita would hit the nightclubs and trendy bars at night and sleep until noon the next day.

The fire continued to burn within her, although she could not have identified it, and might not even have known it was there. But she knew she was a long way from Fargo. More than geographically she was a long way from Fargo. After six months away from home she "kept in touch" with one postcard — from Miami Beach.

"One lousy postcard! She's really keeping in touch," Erica scornfully commented to her mother the day the card arrived. Erica refused to read it. "I don't have time to read about the grand life she's living," Erica said when her mother handed her the card.

"One of these days she'll come around," Mildred said. "She has to grow up."

"Yeah, well, she's doing it the expensive way. And throwing it right in our faces, too," Erica responded.

"We all grow up differently, don't we?" Mildred offered. She paused, then added, "Sometimes the apple falls a long way from the tree."

"Right, and sometimes the apple gets rotten in the process." Erica didn't enjoy the harsh comments she levelled at her sister. Somehow she wished it could have been different.

Deep down she wished she and Estelle had been much closer as sisters. But it hadn't worked out. Playing with dolls and trotting to school hand in hand was to her stranger than fiction. And at times at night, in the loneliness of her bed, her tears came from a mixture of bitterness and regret.

Two years now passed since Estelle left Fargo for the bright lights, and her money had long since disappeared. She had inherited none of the careful and prudent spending habits of her parents, which was bad enough on its own. But more and more in the past two years her money was being spent on alcohol and drugs, and always in the company of Lolita. They had hit the fast lanes from San Juan, Puerto Rico, to San Francisco. The cost was measured not only in the bundle of money, but also in her health. The alcohol and drugs had interfered with her appetite, and both she and Lolita began to feel the effects.

With the money gone, it was no surprise to them that the fair-weather friends were also gone. And the good times. Eventually they joined the ever-burgeoning population of street people. They were homeless. As the two of them sat in the Salvation Army shelter one evening in San Francisco, Estelle wept softly. She shook her head, as though she didn't quite believe what had happened to her. Coming from a solid hardworking and respectable Fargo family, she was now no different from the nameless homeless people who roamed the streets by day and slept in shelters at night. It was the first time in nearly two years that she took the time to evaluate her life. "It was quite a trip, wasn't it?" she said, partly to Lolita and partly to the wall. "I wonder if I might have grown up a bit and gotten it all out of my system."

"Gotten what out?" Lolita asked, not really expecting an answer.

"The fire. I think I had something burning in me," Estelle answered. "Now it's almost out, and I've got nothing left."

After a long pause Lolita offered, "You've got a mother and a sister."

"I wonder if I do?" Estelle asked somewhat wistfully.

"Why don't you find out?" Lolita challenged.

A longer pause, and then, "Will you come with me if I try to go home?" Estelle asked, partly accepting the challenge.

"When do we leave?" Lolita shot right back.

"Let's hit the road tomorrow morning!" Estelle nearly shouted, in a voice that showed some hope and expectation for the first time in months. "Maybe ... maybe Momma will give us a job as janitors in the plant," she laughed. They exchanged high fives before they sacked out on the Salvation Army cots. A few of the other homeless observing them wondered what was going on that made these two seem suddenly so cheerful.

They hitchhiked for three days before they got to Spokane. From there Estelle used some of the few pennies she had earned washing dishes in San Francisco to send a postcard to her mother — the first in a year. The message was simple and poignant. "I'm coming home — bringing a friend. May I ...?" She couldn't ask any more.

The truck driver who gave them the ride that brought them to Spokane believed their story about going to Fargo, and offered them money to take the bus the rest of the way. A day and a half later when they got off the bus — with a ragged satchel of belongings between them — Estelle could hardly believe that Fargo was so beautiful. The two of them walked the 20 blocks or so to her parental home, the home where she grew up along the Red River, and Mildred was just arriving home for a quick lunch break. Mother and daughter embraced for long moments without saying anything — an embrace that was far more than a perfunctory hello.

"Welcome home, dear," Mildred was finally able to stammer.

"I love you, Momma, and I'm sorry for all the grief I may have caused you," Estelle said through her tears.

"I love you, too, Estelle dear. You're home, and that's all that matters now," Mildred said, mascara smearing her face.

"Momma, this is Lolita. We're ... close ... companions." Estelle didn't quite know how to tell her mother. "Momma, we're lesbians."

To Estelle's stunned surprise, her mother said, "So? You're my daughter, aren't you?" Another long embrace, after which she gave Lolita an equally long embrace. Then suddenly, "I'm going to take the afternoon off and help you people get settled in ... are you staying?"

"We'd like to ... if we may," Estelle offered. "But Momma, don't interrupt your ..."

Mildred interrupted, "Oh poo! I own the company, and I can take time off if I want in order to welcome you home. Let's get you both cleaned up. And what about a clothes buying spree? Would you like that?"

By late afternoon Estelle and Lolita were dressed in bright new outfits that did justice to their natural good looks. When they came down from the guest room, Mildred offered, "I'd like to have a party for you two — would you like that? We could invite your cousins and old friends and the neighbors ... what about it?"

"Well, fine, Momma, but ..." Estelle began.

"No buts about it — let's have it Saturday night. Erica will be coming home from a business trip some time Saturday, and she should be just in time for it." And Mildred called her favorite caterer even before she knew how many people would be attending.

By the time Erica arrived home Saturday evening, the party was in full swing. She was puzzled. "What's going on?" she asked the caterer when she came into the kitchen from the garage.

"Your mother ordered a big bash — it's in celebration of Estelle coming home. I heard she came home Wednesday with a friend. Your mother's expecting you."

"Oh swell," Erica said with no enthusiasm. "She goes away for two years and blows all her money, now she comes home and Mom throws a party for her. Well, I'm going to the office; I've got better things to do than attend a party for a spoiled brat."

The caterer breathed a soft sigh and shook his head, knowing there would be trouble ahead. When Mildred came into the kitchen, she asked the caterer, "Didn't I see Erica drive in a few minutes ago? Where is she? Does she know Estelle is home?"

"She went to the office, Mildred, and yes, she knows Estelle is home," the caterer said in as few words as he could muster.

"Well, if anyone asks for me, tell them I'll be back soon," Mildred said as she left for the office.

"Erica," Mildred said as she walked into Erica's office, which bore a sign that said President, "I know how you feel, but Estelle has asked about you ever since she got home. I'm sure she'd love to see you."

Erica asked, "I hear she's got a friend with her. Who is it, some guy she's been shacking up with?"

"No," Mildred was hesitant. "It's a woman ... Lolita. Estelle says they are both lesbians. I don't know much about that, but I do know she'll still my daughter and still your sister."

Erica was a bit jolted. "Oh swell. That should add to our family reputation in this square town." Neither spoke for a moment. Erica tried to hide her tears. "I don't know if I want to see her." She was crying softly. She paused and took several breaths. Neither woman looked at each other for a few painful moments. Through her tears Erica said, "She wrapped Daddy around her little finger for years ... she probably blew the money he left for her education. She was gone for two years, during which time she sent you two lousy postcards. And now she comes home and wants to be the belle of the ball. It stinks, Momma. It stinks!"

Quietly Mildred said, "The party was my idea, Erica, not hers," in defense of Estelle.

"Well, that doesn't make it any easier for me to join in. I've been holding down the fort here ever since Daddy died — and how many parties have I had?" She was sorry she said that, but it was out. She couldn't retrieve it.

"I thank God every day and night for your being here," Mildred assured. "You have been my strength these years. I do celebrate your presence. Maybe I should have celebrated it in a more obvious manner. The party tonight is not a celebration of where or what Estelle has been, but that she has found herself and is back."

"Momma, I need a hug," Erica said. They joined in a long and tearful embrace.

Blind In One Eye . . .

Parallel Parable: Luke 16:19-31
The Rich Man And Lazarus

    The Downtown Club was an old and well-established bastion for the shakers and movers in Dallas, Texas. That's what it was called — The Downtown Club. Not a fancy or imaginative name, but one had to be well-heeled and successful in business as a first step to becoming a member. Then there was the matter of being recommended by five long-standing members, plus numerous other prerequisites for joining. Oh, yes, and one had to be of the male gender. The club was one of the last holdouts as a hang-out for men only. How long that would last was anybody's guess, but the members continued their enjoyment of the club and their comrades as though things would go on the same forever.

    Raymond Stump had been a member for a relatively short time by the measures of most members. He had finally passed all the requirements of membership just about 10 years ago. So he was kind of in between being an old timer and a newcomer. But he had long since gained popularity with other members, and was held in high esteem by those who knew him. Ray was a wealthy insurance man who had made it to the top of his profession, both in his professional skills and in the enormous money he made. Dallas had been good to him. And he was relatively good to Dallas.

    Thursday evening was poker night at the club. Members who regularly played poker on that night had leave of their wives and their business worries, and they had a rousing good time on those nights. The chef always prepared a table full of specialties on which they could nibble until well past midnight. Waiters were kept busy mixing and serving drinks to the several tables of players. Most professional players — that is, those who made their living playing — would never consider consuming any alcoholic beverages while playing. It dulled the senses too much. But these guys were not professional poker players. They played as an excuse to spend the night out with the boys. And it wouldn't matter if any of them dropped a couple thousand dollars during the evening. And for those who won that much, it wouldn't make any difference in their bank accounts.

Thursday evening. Poker evening. Along about midnight, when Ray had gotten a bit juiced up, he and the men at his table were more interested in talking and telling jokes than they were in playing serious poker. "Hey guys," Ray raised his voice a bit to try to get his companions' attention. "Listen, listen. I heard this idea at lunch the other day, and it struck my funny bone. One of the guys I was with at lunch said, 'You know what I'd like to do? I'd like to buy a small island in the South Pacific, and build me a big casino where all my friends could come and relax and enjoy themselves. And I'd have a huge neon sign out in front with letters six-feet tall that said To Hell With Poor People!' "

Everyone had a big laugh over that one, including men from some of the other tables. Some nodded their heads as though they wished they had said something that clever. "Ray, you are something else," one of his poker buddies said, laughing and shaking his head.

"Well, hey, it wasn't my idea, you know, but I must confess I rather like the suggestion. The sign! Man, I like the sign! To Hell With Poor People!" More laughter from his buddies. The poker playing came to a standstill at Ray's table as well as a few adjoining tables. Ray's story had tickled the ears of some, but it also brought forward a topic of conversation with which they were all familiar. Poor people. People on welfare. People with the damnable AIDS disease. Unemployed people. Street people. Homeless people.

Their conversation wasn't the sort that expressed sympathy and concern for those people. It was rather the drag that they were on society. And everyone had their favorite bad words to bring forward about the poor. "Hell, most of these people could get work if they wanted it. The trouble is, most of them are too damned lazy. They're a leech on the rest of us," one of the men began.

And that started it. A cascade of familiar words — almost like negative proverbs — about the poor and homeless. "I tell you, it burns me when some of these people drive up in a Cadillac to get their food stamps!" one fella said, as though he was the first one ever to try that line.

The man serving drinks to the table from which that comment came didn't show any sign that he had heard the remark, but he was thinking, "There's no way these folks ever get near enough to a poor person to see whether or not they're pickin' up food stamps. Cadillac my hind end."

Ray jumped into the verbal assault. "Listen, I haven't got anything against poor people, per se ..." Others nodded their heads in somewhat pious agreement. Ray continued, "But I've become pretty much convinced there's no excuse for it in most cases. People can pick themselves up by their bootstraps and improve their lot ... sweeten this drink up for me, will you son?" he said the waiter.

"We're just spending more and more of our tax money on people who don't want to work. That ain't right," another chimed in.

And so it went for another half hour or so. Ray didn't mention that he had indeed picked himself up by his bootstraps, from poverty to enormous wealth. Something in him said he didn't want these wealthy colleagues to know that he had come from dirt poor beginnings. He would rather they just assumed he had always been a man of wealth, that he was from "old money," not "new money." Chances are, however, that they knew he wasn't from an old money family. He considered himself lucky to be accepted into the elite company of old-monied people.

Ray and his five younger brothers were sons of a poor tenant farmer near Perham, Minnesota. Ray was old enough to remember the Depression years on the farm, when there was barely enough food to put on the table. Their father just couldn't improve the family's financial situation as the years rolled by, partly because he had the bad luck to be renting a farm that had mediocre soil, and partly because during the Great Depression prices were so low it didn't make any difference even if he did produce good crops. Ray never could figure out why it was called the "Great" Depression — there wasn't anything great about it in his eyes.

Nor was there anything great or noble about being poor. From the time of his early teen years Ray began to resent his poor background. Although many other people in those years were low on the economic scale, Ray considered it a curse to be poor. Because of their poverty, the family never had more than basic bland food; and clothes for the six boys always looked as though they were ready for the rag bag. He would some day escape the poverty cycle, he vowed to himself many times over.

It couldn't happen too soon as far as he was concerned. So he dropped out of school following his junior year in high school, ostensibly to make a little money to help the family finances, but in his own mind it was the beginning of his plan to make money — lots of it — so he would never again have to suffer the disgrace of poverty. In his eyes it was definitely a disgrace.

Ray worked a variety of jobs in his late teen years, and eventually wound up in his early 20s working for an insurance agent. In spite of his not having finished high school, he soon began learning enough about the insurance business to study for and get his certification as an agent. It wasn't long before he felt this would be his path to riches. And he was right. He became a star salesman and after a time established his own agency. He was on the way to stardom in his field.

He needed a bigger field of operation — and Texas provided such a field. It was the late '40s, and after some investigation, he decided that Dallas, Texas, was the place where he needed to be to cash in on the lucrative field of insurance. He risked what he had built up in his own agency, and moved to Dallas to start from scratch. Within a decade he was a prosperous insurance executive with a large stable of salespeople and an income that seemed it would never end. He had left his poverty behind, as far behind as he could leave it — geographically, financially, and psychologically. In his mind poverty was still a curse, a curse which he thought most people could avoid if they really tried, as he had. And as he had succeeded.

Ray's life was not all smooth. The long hours he spent building up his business had the effect of distancing himself from his wife and three children. The divorce which followed was devastating to him, more from the status standpoint than that the family had broken up. And it meant more time spent at the club to fill the few hours of free time he could carve out each week. Meanwhile he had helped his five brothers, one by one, to get through college, and each of them was on a track similar to Ray's. A successful attorney, a doctor, a real estate broker and two younger brothers who would climb the ladder of success in some field or another as oldest brother Ray would advance them whatever grub stake they needed to get on their way out of the poverty cycle. And that was indeed commendable.

Friday on his way to work, Ray ordered his chauffeur, "Will you please take some other route this morning? I hate going past that food kitchen where all those street people are waiting for free food." He didn't know why he hated it, he just didn't want to have anything to do with the scene. "And Willy, let's stop at the United Way office. I need to make sure everything's going right for this year's drive." Ray was chairperson of the annual United Way drive this year, and he was determined it was going to go over the top more than in previous years. Ray was good at raising money. He had been chairperson of the capital funds drive for their new church building a few years ago, a drive that went far beyond what the pastor and church council members had dared to hope. Ray could raise money for church and for United Way. He knew that United Way assisted many poor and impoverished people, and he was glad for that — as long as he could keep a safe distance from anyone who was actually in need.

He was particularly self-conscious in the presence of poor people, didn't know how to act. So it seemed best to him simply to stay as far away as possible from any contact with the poor. "To hell with poor people!" still found a silent welcome home in the back recesses of his mind. He didn't know why. The contradiction in him was that he felt good about raising money for the poor, even though he believed most of them didn't need to be poor. And he didn't want to get close to any poor people.

But then there was Larry. No one knew his last name. But Larry somehow always seemed to find his way to the entrance to Ray's office. He wasn't any trouble. He was just there. He was a street person, had no home, was in obvious poor health, and always seemed to be needing a bath. There was no law against Larry loitering around the front entrance to Ray's office, but Ray wished there were a law. In fact at times he tried to get the police to shoo Larry away. But a few days later Larry would be back, watching overweight Ray, in his $1,200 Italian suits, enter his office, and he'd be there when Ray came out to do lunch with his friends or customers. Larry was a pain in the butt to Ray. If someone had asked Ray why that was so, he wouldn't have been able to come up with a logical answer, but he knew deep down that he didn't like having Larry there, practically on his office doorstep. If he had gone to a counselor about it, maybe Ray would have discovered that Larry was too much of a reminder of Ray's own roots. Roots of poverty. The curse of poverty. So Ray passed him by nearly every day as though Larry didn't exist. It was the only thing Ray could do, because there was no way he could become involved with one of these hundreds of street people. Ignore them, Ray said to himself. I'm doing my part with my work in United Way. I can't deal with individuals.

But Larry weighed on his mind more than Ray realized. He could put him out of sight for a time, but in the back of his mind Larry was there, nagging him. The silent nagging culminated in a traumatic dream Ray had one night. Or was it a nightmare? Whatever it was, it bothered Ray for several days, to the point that he sought the help of a counselor, someone to whom he could relate this stupid dream.

"I dreamed I had died!" Ray said, beads of sweat forming on his forehead. The counselor was properly calm and unmoved.

"Well, tell me more," cool counselor invited.

"I don't know ... this sounds crazy!" Ray continued.

"Most dreams sound crazy when we wake up," counselor responded.

"But I was in hell!" Ray almost shouted. "Great balls of fire, I was in hell!"

"All right, so it was a dream," the counselor almost smiled. "Just tell me how much you can remember."

"Well, there was this guy named Larry ... Larry is a bum, a street person, who hangs out in front of my office. And there was Larry off in the distance. I think he was in heaven. Lord, I was scared, because I was in hell. And what was that street bum doing in heaven, for God's sake?"

"Was there anything else?"

"Yeah. There was St. Peter, or someone, I don't know who it was. And he was over there with Larry, in heaven. I asked him what the deal was, that I was in this God-forsaken place, and Larry was apparently in heaven. After all I had done for the church and United Way and Lord knows what else, what was that no-good bum doing in heaven, and I'm in hell?"

"What did St. Peter, or whoever, say?"

Ray paused a while before answering, softly and slowly, "He said I'd had my day, my good times and all, and that Larry was one of the forgotten people. I guess he implied that I blew it. I don't know, I was confused. I'm still confused."

"Is that it?"

"No, I asked the guy, whoever he was, if he could send a message to my brothers, maybe send Larry! — because they are following the same track as I was. If I blew it, maybe my brothers could be warned, somehow ..." His voice trailed off. "I don't know exactly what I was saying or what I was asking." Ray paused as if trying to recall the dream. "The guy said that they have the same chance I had to hear the message, whatever that meant."

"Do you know what it meant?"

"No, how should I know what it meant? It was a dream. It was unreal." Ray paused, then continued, more subdued, "I thought, hey, if someone were to come back from the dead — okay, so let's continue this stupid, unreal dream — if someone were to come back from the dead, my brothers at least would be spared the hell that I was in."

"And ...?"

"And the guy said if they didn't hear the message, they wouldn't pay attention even to someone coming back from the dead."

"That's it?"

"Yeah, that's it. Confusing, isn't it? I don't know even now if I'm awake or dreaming."

Perfect In Every Way

Parallel Parable: Luke 18:9-14
Pharisee And Tax Collector

Karl Schmidt loved to sing, and for good reason. His rich baritone had been a lead voice in the church choir ever since he graduated from high school more than 30 years ago. And like so many singers, sometimes a tune would get stuck in his mind and vocal chords and he couldn't dislodge it, much to the dismay, at times, of his wife Ellen.

Tonight was one of those times. "Kids, what's the matter with kids today?" Karl was singing for all the neighborhood to hear. "Karl, it's 11:00 at night, for cryin' out loud! The neighbors will be calling us about your singing."

"Oh, they love my voice," Karl said without taking Ellen's complaint too seriously.

Earlier in the evening Karl and Ellen had joined friends from the church and attended the stage production of *Bye Bye Birdie* at the local community theater. The song from that musical that stuck in Karl's mind he was now singing with all the gusto of his wonderful baritone voice. "Let the neighbors hear, it will probably do them some good," Karl suggested. But he was most likely just as interested in hearing his own voice belt out the tune. The lyrics continued, "Why can't they be like we were — perfect in every way — oh, what's the matter with kids today?"

"I like those lyrics," Karl said to no one in particular as he relaxed with a beer.

"I'm afraid you take those words more literally than you ought to," Ellen commented. "I'm not so sure that we were any better in our youth than the kids are today."

"Oh right, gimme a break!" Karl sputtered through his beer. "We didn't have all those drugs and rebellion and Lord knows what all in our day!"

But Ellen wasn't backing down. "I read once," she said, "that the ancient Greeks and Romans used to complain the same way about the youth, and how they were so much worse than previous generations. People always think the old days were better."

"Well, for my money they were," Karl continued. "Take the high school kids of today — I mean wanting condoms handed out in school, for heaven's sake!"

With a knowing smile on her face Ellen proposed, "Maybe we should have had condoms handed out to us our senior year in high school, and we wouldn't have had such a hurry-up marriage — and a six-month preemie who weighed in at nearly nine pounds."

Karl ignored that reference. He knew she had scored a point. And yet Karl couldn't completely abandon the idea that things were better "back in the old days," although he wasn't all that old yet. Just a bit more than 50. There was something in Karl's attitude that seemed to say, "When I grew up, things were better." Or maybe it was the way he grew up, he wasn't sure what it was. But deep down inside he rather believed he came out a better person than most, although that wasn't the kind of sentiment he would venture to let escape. But it formed a part of his character.

Searching for additional ammunition, Karl said, "I'm just glad I was raised in a Christian home and learned how to support the church and do my part ..."

"Honey, I'm not saying you shouldn't be proud of your upbringing or of your heritage. That's fine. It's just that at times you project a feeling that others don't quite measure up," Ellen said, trying to get some perspective into this nonproductive discussion.

"... and I'm not ashamed to thank God for the kind of life I live." It was as though he hadn't been listening to Ellen's words of support. "Compared to our Catholic neighbor Hugo, I might be eligible for sainthood," he chuckled at the thought of it.

"Well now, don't get on Hugo's case again," Ellen responded with some irritation mixed with sympathy. "We all know Hugo has his problems ..."

"Yeah, right. He's got problems all right. You can tell the problems he's got by the amount of whiskey bottles in his garbage — doesn't even recycle like we do."

Hugo McPhail lived next door to the Schmidts. Karl was right about Hugo in some respects. Hugo was on the bottle too much of the time. He had switched jobs so many times even he had lost count. He had lost his wife and children years ago because of his drinking problem, and he just didn't seem able to muster the strength and willpower to get out of his rut. A rut that was leading nowhere but downhill.

As he sat alone this evening in his messy house, half watching an old movie and nursing his fourth drink, Hugo repeated to himself words he had said often in the past. "Let's face it, I blew it. I screwed up everything I ever put my hand to." He half laughed as he said, "Lord, it's bad, ain't it? Look at this wasted life ..." In spite of the booze, his analytical mind still worked well. "Lord, he said slowly, as though for once he might actually be addressing God, "I really botched it, didn't I? Is there a second or third chance for guys like me?"

At the Schmidt house the debate continued, "Hugo ran around on Sarah long before he had a drinking problem," Karl intoned. "And he neglected the kids something fierce."

"We don't know all that's been going on in his life. I think we just need to be less judgmental of others," Ellen again trying for better perspective.

"You're always defending him. Why do you do that?" Karl pleaded. "I mean, everyone knows he's a failure. And God knows he hasn't set foot in church in 25 years. I don't agree with his Catholic teachings, but at least he ought to go to mass once in a while. Or maybe, better yet, to confession!"

"I defend him because he's a human being, and needs our help much more than he needs our criticism," Ellen protested.

"Well, you ought to thank God I'm not like him ... I do, whenever I pray," Karl said, knowing he shouldn't have added that last part, because it gave Ellen some ammunition.

"I don't think it's right to thank God you're not like other people. God knows who you are. A little humility wouldn't hurt, you know," she scolded.

But the discussion was essentially over. Karl chugged the rest of his beer, belched, and launched into singing those same words again, "Why can't they be like we were — perfect in every way, oh, what's the matter with kids today?" His sonorous baritone almost rattled the dishes. He loved that song. Man, did he love that song! But it wasn't just a catchy tune for him. He enjoyed the lyrics far too much. It suited his mood. It suited his philosophy. To Ellen's distress, the song seemed to reflect far too accurately Karl's evaluation of others — compared to himself.

Next door Hugo was about ready for bed. But in a departure from his usual bedtime routine, which would have been one more drink, he sat mumbling half aloud. "Well, Lord, where shall I start?" he asked, not knowing for sure if God was listening. He had been reading an article about Alcoholics Anonymous. Before he went to sleep he thought he might be addressing God, "I've got no place to go but up, right Lord?"

www.ingramcontent.com/pod-product-compliance
Lightning Source LLC
Chambersburg PA
CBHW060846050426
42453CB00008B/848